CHILDREN OF POVERTY

STUDIES ON THE EFFECTS
OF SINGLE PARENTHOOD,
THE FEMINIZATION OF POVERTY,
AND HOMELESSNESS

edited by

STUART BRUCHEY
UNIVERSITY OF MAINE

A GARLAND SERIES

RUNAWAY YOUTH

STRESS, SOCIAL SUPPORT, AND ADJUSTMENT

JON BRADLEY

GARLAND PUBLISHING, INC.
NEW YORK & LONDON / 1997

Library of Congress Cataloging-in-Publication Data

Bradley, Jon
    Runaway youth : stress, social support, and adjustment / Jon
Bradley.
        p.   cm. — (Children of poverty)
    Includes bibliographical references and index.
    ISBN 0-8153-2798-6 (alk. paper)
    1. Runaway teenagers—New York (State)—New York—
Social conditions. 2. Homeless youth—New York (State)—New
York—Social conditions. 3. Runaway teenagers—Services for—
New York (State)—New York. 4. Homeless youth—Services for—
New York (State)—New York. 5. Shelters for the homeless—New
York (State)—New York. I. Title. II. Series.
HV1437.N5B73 1997
362.74—dc21
                                                        96-37854

Printed on acid-free, 250-year-life paper
Manufactured in the United States of America

Contents

List of Tables

Acknowledgments

I have been able to complete the book due to support from many sources. Resources from the National Institute of Mental Health available through the HIV Center for Clinical and Behavioral Studies at New York State Psychiatric Institute made this research possible. I thank Brenda McGowan and Mary Jane Rotheram-Borus as well as many other friends and colleagues for their help and encouragement. The support of my family in New York and in Portland has been invaluable.

This work is dedicated to my parents, Wesley and Cheryl Bradley, my wife, Blanca Santiago, and my brother Lance, who was there for me from the start.

Runaway Youth

I
Introduction

HISTORY OF THE PROBLEM

Homeless and runaway adolescents are not unique to modern society. Youth who left home and children who were victims of abuse, neglect, or exploitation all appear in nineteenth century literature. In the history of the United States, runaways and those who were homeless were among our founders and took part in settling the western states (Libertoff, 1980). During the Great Depression of the 1930s, many teenagers left home, often with the approval of struggling parents. In fact, transient youth were a target of the Federal Relief Administration in 1933.

Attempts to intervene with runaway and homeless youth have increased since the 1960s as this phenomenon has been recognized as a growing reflection of family instability and of the problems of children and teenagers in our society. Shelters were established to provide emergency housing and crisis intervention to these youth. Perceived by some in the 1960s as part of the "hippie flower children" phenomenon (Moses, 1978) running away has proven to be a complex and persistent social problem.

In 1974, concern about adolescents leaving home led to the enactment of the Runaway Youth Act, Title III of the Juvenile Justice and Delinquency Prevention Act (JDPA, pp. 93-415). This law funded shelters around the United States to provide emergency services to runaways. Responding to concerns that many runaway youth were in fact homeless, the Runaway Youth Act was renamed the Runaway and Homeless Youth Act in 1980. In 1984 it was further amended and renamed the Missing, Runaway and Homeless Youth Act. Federal funds provide support for the maintenance of a network of emergency shelters throughout the United States. Additional funds have been directed toward the development of new approaches to specific problems of runaway and homeless youth, such as suicide, substance abuse, or lack of vocational skills. Several states have passed legislation which supports shelters and services to runaway and homeless youth. In 1978, New York State enacted its Runaway and Homeless Youth Act, which provides funds for runaway shelters and governs how shelters should be operated (Executive Law ~~532 et seq.). State funding continues and the New York Runaway and Homeless Youth Act has been amended to create funding for longer term transitional shelters for homeless youth.

In the past three decades much has been learned about the reasons teenagers run away and about the family and institutional problems that contribute to homelessness. Program models for providing emergency shelter, street outreach, and independent or transitional living have emerged to address the problems of these adolescents. Coalitions and networks of runaway and homeless youth service providers advocate for the special needs and concerns of this growing population. While still under-served by under-funded programs, runaway and homeless youth have become the focus of national attention in recent years.

Estimating the number of runaway and homeless youth has proven difficult due to the transient nature of the population, and differing definitions of homelessness. Those estimates that do exist confirm that the problem is great and the numbers large. In 1982, the number of runaway and homeless youth was reported to be between 733,000 and 1,300,000 (Chelimsky, 1982). In 1984, the Department of Health and Human Services estimated that the number of runaway and homeless youth between the ages of 10 and 17 was more than one million each year (DHHS, 1984). The Children's Defense Fund, in 1988, estimated 1.5 million homeless youth ages 11 to 18. In 1990 the National Network of Runaway and Youth Services estimated that there were between 1 and 1.5 million runaway and homeless youth a year (Nationa Network of Runaway and Youth Services, 1990). Cities surveyed by the U.S. Conference of Mayors reported that 4% of all homeless persons were unaccompanied youth (Solarz, 1988). Federally supported programs served about 333,000 youth in 1987, although one recent report on homeless youth estimated that only one in twelve youth is served in federally funded shelters (Yates et al., 1988).

Much of the literature on runaways has focused on causes of runaway episodes and on differentiating types of runaways based on reasons for leaving home. (Homer, 1973; Brennan, 1980; Adams, Gullota, and Clancy, 1980; Jones, 1988; Shane, 1989; Crespi and Sabatelli, 1993). Several social scientists have developed paradigms and taxonomies of runaway behavior (Cherry, 1993; Zide and Cherry,

1992) Jones, 1988; Nye, 1980; Brennan, 1980; English, 1973). Much of this literature is anecdotal and reveals unsubstantiated bias. Other research is based on extremely limited samples or samples which cannot be viewed as representative of runaway and homeless youth in general. Indeed, many of the statistics used to describe these youth come from specific agency evaluations and numbers given by programs to funding sources.

Clearly, runaways are a diverse and largely unexplored population who are defined by an act rather than a specific set of problems or experiences. Although the causes of runaway behavior are complex, perhaps it is best viewed as a means of coping with and responding to problems in living situations, problems with family, friends, or the institutions in which adolescents grow. Efforts to discover the impact of the runaway experience, of living on the streets, and of adapting to a lifestyle of instability have been limited, but should assist in developing more effective intervention strategies.

THE CURRENT STUDY

This study focuses on a sample of runaway and homeless youth in two shelters in New York City in order to discover whether residential instability, stress, and social supports are related to adjustment and problem behaviors in this population of youth at high risk. It evaluates the impact of changing living situations and leaving home on the formation of peer friendship networks, on the continuation of relationships with parents or adult guardians, and ultimately on how runaways might do in adjusting to the demands of adulthood.

Rather than attempt to understand these youth by scrutinizing differences within the population that help to categorize runaway youth, this study explores three key sets of variables across a runaway sample: residential instability, stress, and social supports. These variables may shed light on the adjustment and behaviors of this population of youth, and improve understanding of how the experience of running away or being homeless affects individual youth. Literature in adolescent development and social work practice points toward the need to understand the complex interaction of life history, social environment, and development (Hamburger, 1974; Germaine and Gitterman, 1980. The variables explored in this study are drawn from research on the impact of social experience on individuals.

Assessment measures were developed based on previous research, theoretical soundness, and social work practice wisdom.The sample, drawn from youth seeking shelter, was anticipated to be relatively homogeneous in several of the key variables explored in this study. For example, it was expected that compared to a broad sample of adolescents, this population would show clustering in high rates of instability, maladjustment and behavior problems. Thus, findings which prove to be statistically significant in this sample would be evidence of a powerful relationship and might, indeed, be rare. Therefore, it is important to emphasize that this study also presents an opportunity to explore and to describe for the first time the stability, stress, social supports, adjustment and problem behaviors of runaway youth compared to other adolescent populations. In particular, social supports and measures of stress have received little focus in research about runaway and homeless youth.

In recent years several studies of runaway youth have attempted to develop psychosocial profiles and evaluate the psychological adjustment of runaway and homeless adolescents (Shaffer and Caton, 1983; Rotheram and Bradley, 1991; Rotheram, Koopman, and Bradley, 1989; DeMan et al, 1994; DeMan et al 1993; Kashubeck et al, 1994). However, little work has addressed the impact of runaway experiences themselves on these youth or the state of the runaways' world at the time they seek services.

Literature on adolescence consistently emphasizes the importance of parents and peers in adjustment and in the development of values. Studies of foster children and others who have lived in many different settings have documented the impact of inconsistent parenting and changing living situations on teenagers' adjustment (Fanshel and Shinn, 1989; Proch and Taber, 1987; Pardeck, 1982;). Yet little is known about the impact of runaway episodes, of periodic homelessness, and of moving from place to place on the youth who seek runaway shelter services.

Shelters that work with runaway and homeless youth face the challenge of developing a service plan which includes addressing mental health, family, substance abuse, and health issues as necessary. Practice experience in these settings indicates that many of these youth are isolated, risk taking, angry, and hopeless. Some have been through "the system" and have no family or friends, only "associates" on the streets. Others have just started to run away and are still connected to parents or family members. Does the experience of continuous running away remove hope, self-esteem, and positive supports from these youth? Can beginning to understand the impact of such stressful experiences as homelessness and institutionalization on these youth shed any light on future program directions? Do social supports from parents and/or from peers appear to hold any keys to helping the more troubled youth become stable and independent adults?

This study is based on a sample of intakes into runaway programs in New York City. The study represents a unique opportunity to conduct extensive interviews with youth who are receiving services in a runaway shelter, an opportunity made possible by a large study of which the author was project director. The relationship between this study and the larger research project is discussed in greater detail in Chapter 3.

Baseline interviews in two runaway programs were conducted as part of a longitudinal research project aimed at developing an intervention which would prove effective in decreasing risk for HIV infection among runaway and homeless youth. The interviews, which were administered at the time of intake into the shelter programs, provided detailed information relating to current risk behaviors and psychosocial factors that might relate to increased risk. They also provided a unique opportunity to look at critical aspects of runaway and homeless youth's experiences, social interactions, and current coping patterns. Four key sets of variables are explored separately and in relationship to each other: residential instability, acute stress, social supports, and adjustment and behavior problems.

Residential instability, along with measures of stressful life events (acute stress) are viewed as indicators of stress in this study. Residential instability is based on a set of measures aimed at understanding youth's runaway and placement history, measures which may indicate a type of chronic stress experienced by these youth. It is derived from information about past living situations such as number of runaway episodes, age of first running away, length of time since being at home, and number of different types of living situations. Residential instability in this study does not evaluate the emotional content of family relationships or the details of changing living situations as these cannot be accurately obtained in one interview with youth who are often distrustful. In addition, this information about relationships might overlap with measures of current social supports and relationships.

Acute stress is viewed as recent events which result in a stressed state. It is measured by assessing the number of negatively experienced life changes or events which youth have experienced in the past three months. Acute stress is viewed as a key means of understanding the impact of recent change and life problems on individuals and is measured utilizing an adaptation of the Life Events Checklist (Johnson and McCutcheon, 1980).

Social supports refers to resources available to an individual through other people or groups of people. This term has generally been broadly and vaguely defined and, in fact, represents a number of different concepts. In this study, specific qualities of the network of people who supply assistance to the runaway youth are evaluated. These include satisfaction with supports, the number of people in the network, the number of peers in the network, and the presence or absence of parents or adult relatives as well as information about the degree of substance use among network members.

Adjustment is an indication of distress which has been shown to decrease coping and to interfere with social interactions. In this sample of runaways, individual adjustment is measured by scales for depression and self-esteem. Problem behaviors are measured by a scale for conduct disorder as well as by measures of drug use and sexual risk taking.

The primary goal of this study was to assess the correlation among variables related to stress (instability and stressful life events), social supports, and adjustment (see Figure 1). Theories of stress and of the possible buffering effects of social supports on stress led to the design, which includes a regression analysis including residential instability, social supports, and adjustment and behaviors.

Data analysis was also designed to describe current patterns and examine relationships among the specific measures used to evaluate residential instability, and stress, supports, and adjustment. Information derived from the data provided an opportunity to compare characteristics of this runaway and homeless youth sample with other populations of youth.

BACKGROUND OF THE STUDY

The potential importance of social experience in determining health and mental health and in influencing the nature of coping efforts was recognized by the developers of crisis theory (Lazarus, 1966; Mechanic, 1974; White, 1974; Rapaport, 1965; Rapoport, 1965; Golan, 1978) and by those studying the effects of stress (Seyle, 1976; Holmes and Rahe, 1967; Dohrenwrend and Dohrenwrend, 1974; Dohrenwrend, 1969). Social work practice incorporated an understanding of the social environment as an important area for intervention from its beginning. However, in the last 20 years there has been greater recognition of the importance of social supports and informal networks (Swenson, 1979; Collins and Pancoast, 1976; Kelly and Kelly, 1985; Schilling, 1987).

In the 1970s sociologists and psychologists became interested in the importance of social supports when influential works by Caplan, Cassel, and Cobb provided a theoretical base for many researchers (Caplan, 1974; Cassel, 1976; Cobb, 1976). In subsequent years, there have been many studies which support the relationship of social supports to physical illness and psychological disorder. Most of these studies have been with adult populations, although there is a small body of literature focusing on children and adolescents (Sandler, 1980; Barrera, 1981; Cauce, Felner, and Primavera, 1982; Burke and Weir, 1978; Gad and Johnson, 1980; Compass et al., 1986; McGowan and Kohn, 1990). While there is clear evidence that social supports can play a role in adjustment, findings have been preliminary and often difficult to compare because of shifting definitions of social supports. In addition, while several of these studies have focused on youth considered at high risk due to socio-economic status, and ethnic and neighborhood characteristics, few have evaluated the importance of social supports as a determinant of behavior among a sample of youth already engaged in troubling behavior.

Research with similar New York City runaway and homeless youth has verified that this is a population with multiple problems and high rates of adjustment problems. According to the New York City Youth Board, there are an estimated 20,000 runaway and/or homeless youth in New York City on any given day (New York City Youth Board Estimates, 1988). Based on program statistics and research findings (Shaffer and Caton, 1983; Rotheram and Bradley, 1991) more than one half of these youth are indeed homeless, having no stable environment to which to return. Studies have found that more than 30% of these youth are involved in the child welfare system and are running from or have been discharged from placements (Citizen's Committee for the Children of New York, 1983).

These adolescents have extremely high rates of depression and conduct problems (Shaffer and Caton, 1983; Rotheram and Bradley, 1991). It is estimated that 85% of these youth are sexually active; 85% use illegal drugs; 70% of the boys and 45% of the girls have dropped out or been expelled from school; and more than 20% have been involved in prostitution at some time (Rotheram, Koopman, and Bradley, 1989). Many youth report never using condoms and consistent safer sex is almost nonexistent. The combination of high rates of substance abuse and high rates of sexual risk taking place runaways at great risk for HIV infection (Koopman et al, 1994).

Social support variables are emphasized as a possible area for targeting intervention as well as a way of better understanding the effects of chronic instability or runaway experiences. In social work, informal supports have been emphasized as a crucial area with which practitioners must work. Despite agreement about the importance of informal supports, the strategic use of informal support networks in populations at high risk is still not clear in social work practice,. Schilling (1987), in discussing the limitations of social supports concludes:

> Without question, social supports can be a positive bond benefiting provider and recipient. In other circumstances, the costs of supports may outweigh the benefits. In still other situations, social supports may have untoward effects on providers, recipients, and others. Current knowledge suggests that social supports remains a vague and inadequately defined concept. Because of their universal appeal and congruence with the present political climate, social support concepts may be precipitously translated into social work practice. (p. 29)

Clinicians may be correct to assume that lack of peer supports can increase the likelihood of depression or low self esteem. However, there is evidence that increased peer supports can also relate to substance abuse in certain populations (Vik, Grizzle, and Brown, 1992;

Hawkins and Fraser, 1984). The relationship between social support variables and adjustment is not yet clear. Studies must concentrate on specific populations, well-defined components of social supports and clarity about the ways in which adjustment will be measured.

This study looks at residential instability, a specific social experience common among runaway and homeless youth. If residential instability appears to relate to changes in available social supports and affects adjustment, clinical social workers and program planners will be supported in efforts of early intervention. Preventing future changes in living situation and associated stress experienced by youth is supported as a target for programs and resources. Furthermore, evidence that residential instability is a significant variable in the adjustment of these youth reinforces the importance of understanding the experiences which youth have in various family and institutional settings. If specific characteristics of social support networks appear to buffer the effects of residential instability (chronic stress) or life events (acute stressors), a direction for possible interventions with runaway adolescents becomes clearer.

Runaway and homeless youth by definition have troubled histories and can be expected to be relatively unstable and to have inadequate, inconsistent social supports and many adjustment and behavior problems. Significant findings in this population which is extreme in each of these areas, may also indicate directions for research with more general adolescent populations. How important are specific social support variables in adolescent populations? Does this study find any evidence that social supports act as a buffer, even in a skewed adolescent sample?

INITIAL HYPOTHESES AND RESEARCH QUESTIONS

Because relatively little is known about runaway and homeless youth, this study will present basic data relating to residential instability, stress, social supports, and adjustment while testing hypotheses about the relationships among these variables (see Figure 1). The primary hypotheses of the study posit the following:

1. Residential instability as a measure of a chronic stressor influences youth's social support networks, their response to acute stress, and their adjustment and behaviors. Increased residential instability relates to decreased social supports,

increased stressful events, and increased behavior problems and maladjustment.

2. Social supports act as a buffer to the impact of residential instability on adjustment and behavior problems.

In addition to the basic hypotheses, there are numerous research questions raised by the study's exploration of residential stability, stress, social supports and adjustment variables in a relatively rare sample of extremely high risk youth. These questions form the foundation of the data analysis as well as the basis from which to evaluate the central hypotheses of this study. The research questions are detailed in this section of Chapter 1.

1. Do the following historical measures appear related and potentially form meaningful variables for instability and chronic stress?
   - Number of runaway episodes
   - Age of first running away
   - Length of time since last at home
   - Number of types of different placements
   - Homelessness
   - Experience of institutional living

2. Is residential instability associated with measures of stressful life events or acute stress in this population?

3. What do the social support networks of runaway and homeless youth look like in terms of the following variables?
   - Total network size
   - Number of peers in the network
   - Types of social support activities
   - Youth's satisfaction with support activities
   - Youth's need for support activities
   - Norms in the support network regarding drug abuse?
     a. Are there differences between the social support networks of male and female runaways?
     b. Do specific characteristics of these youth's support networks appear highly related to other key network variables?

4. What patterns emerge in terms of the adjustment and problem behaviors of this sample of troubled youth as indicated by the following variables?
   - Depression

- Self-esteem
- Conduct problems
- Drug use
- Sexual risk taking

    a. Are there differences in the patterns of adjustment and behavior problems between male and female runaways?

    b. Do various adjustment and behavior problem measures appear significantly related in this population?

5. Do residential instability (chronic stress) and life events stress appear associated with specific social support network characteristics?

    a. Do stress variables affect the size, members, or norms of the network?

    b. Are there differences in the relationship between stress and social supports between runaway boys and girls?

6. Do instability (chronic stress) and life events stress appear associated with indicators of adjustment and behavior problems among runaways?

    a. Do stress measures relate to some adjustment variables and behavior problems more than others in this population?

    b. Are there differences in the relationship between stress and adjustment and behavior problems between runaway boys and girls?

7. Do specific characteristics of runaway youth's social support networks appear related to adjustment?

    a. Do social support variables relate to specific types of adjustment more than others in this population?

    b. Are there differences in the relationship between social supports and adjustment between runaway boys and girls?

8. Do social support characteristics appear to buffer the affect of stress (instability and/or life events) on aspects of adjustment in this runaway sample?

OUTLINE OF SUBSEQUENT CHAPTERS

Chapter 2 reviews relevant literature about runaways, stress, social supports, and adolescent social and psychological development. It provides the background and theoretical base for the current research and further specifies beginning hypotheses.

Chapter 3 describes the methodology of the study, describing in detail the design, approach, key concepts, settings, and statistical strategy.

Chapter 4 presents the results of the data analysis. This includes basic demographics: frequencies of major variables; gender and ethnic differences among variables; and relationships between individual measures of residential stability, social supports, and adjustment and behavior problems. Chapter 4 also describes the relationships which emerge among residential instability, stressful life events, social supports, and adjustment and behavior problems. Statistical strategies are detailed in an effort to describe relationships which exist between independent and dependent measures.

Chapter 5 discusses the meaning of the findings of the study which relate to better understanding this high risk adolescent population. How the findings relate to research in adolescent social supports and adjustment and behaviors is also discussed. Finally, particular attention is paid to the degree to which the findings of this study point toward directions for developing effective services for runaway and homeless youth.

II
Literature Review

Chapter 2 begins with a discussion of current knowledge about runaway and homeless youth. This includes a focus on demographics; family problems; residential instability and its impact; and adjustment and behavior problems in this population. Subsequently Chapter 2 reviews current theory and research in the areas of stress and social supports, particularly describing research with adolescents and findings which point to a relationship among stress, social supports, and adjustment.

RUNAWAY AND HOMELESS YOUTH: WHO ARE THEY?

The problem of runaway and homeless youth is serious and complex (American Medical Association, 1989). No longer is running away viewed as a flight to an exciting place or the result of a need to wander. There is general agreement that these youth are running from something, often from a place or a life in which they have felt abused, rejected, and unhappy (Adams et al., 1985; D'Angelo, 1984; DeMan et al 1993; Ferran and Sabitini, 1985; Gordon, 1975; Gullota, 1978; Janus et al 1995; Levine et al., 1986; Mathews and Ilon, 1980; McCormack, Janus, and Burgess, 1986; Pietropino, 1985; Spillane-Grieco, 1984).

In recent years there has been growing interest in youth who live on the streets or in shelters as well as numerous explorations of whether psychological, family, economic or other factors contribute to homelessness among adolescents. In addition to concern about antecedents of homelessness, there has been growing concern about the range of problems which these youth have including sexual exploitation, suicide, HIV infection, and substance abuse.

Despite the interest of the media and the concern expressed by government and communities, there have been limited studies of this population (Hersch, 1989). In fact, they are considered the most understudied subgroup among the current homeless population (Institute of Medicine, 1988). Defining the population of runaway and homeless youth has been a continuing challenge. Their numbers include young teenagers who will return to intact families after one day; teenagers who have been surviving in the streets for weeks and months; youth thrown out of families or institutions; teenagers whose families have lost their homes and must seek emergency shelter; youth escaping victimization; and psychiatrically disturbed youth. The diversity of runaway and homeless youth makes simplistic definitions and descriptions meaningless. Bucy of The National Network of Runaway and Youth Services (1985) differentiates between five overlapping groups: *runaways*, who are away from home at least overnight without parental or guardian consent; *homeless youth*, who have no identified parent or guardian, have left or been urged to leave family or institutional settings, and have no alternative home; *street kids*, who are long-term runaways or homeless youth who have become adept at surviving "on the street," usually by illegal means, and are often not seeking shelter; *throw-aways*, who have been ejected by guardians or parents from a stable living situation; and *system kids*, who have rotated through a variety of placements in the social service and child welfare systems—youth who have run away or been discharged directly to the streets or who have been referred to a runaway program for emergency shelter.

It is important to note that while the National Network of Runaway and Youth Services' grouping of runaways proves helpful in analyzing characteristics of the runaway population and in assessing the service needs of specific youth, these groups are not mutually exclusive. At times youth who are system kids have spent long periods on the streets and, in fact, may be homeless. Most studies of runaways have not differentiated these groups, despite the fact that they represent youth with potentially varied histories and characteristics.

The literature on runaway and homeless youth has major limitations due to methodological biases. These include gathering information from program records and from service providers rather than directly from adolescents themselves; cross-sectional samples that over-report homeless youth in each site and thus over-report factors related to chronic homelessness (Robertson, 1989); surveys that do not account for youth who use multiple services; and finally sampling methods that limit the generalizability of the findings (Rotheram-Borus, Koopman, and Ehrhardt, 1991).

The fact that most data come from atypical samples reflects the scope and variety of the population as well as clear regional and geographic differences. A recent study of runaways who had received services at one of 29 sites in Texas concluded that the runaway problem is ambiguously defined and that no single approach to this diverse group was possible (Gonzalez, 1994). The data most relevant to this study is that collected in urban areas with populations that reflect the mix of runaways, homeless youth, and street kids who gather in the biggest cities. National statistics based on secondary analysis from shelters portray a picture of white, working class runaways which is distinct from the predominately poor minority youth found in New York City programs (Shaffer and Caton, 1984; Rotheram-Borus and Bradley, 1991) or the streetwise, substance abusing adolescents found in Los Angeles (Yates, et al., 1988).

In 1984, Shaffer and Caton conducted an epidemiological survey among runaway and homeless youth in shelters in New York City over a two-week period. Rotheram-Borus and Bradley (1989) collected data on a similar sample of runaway and homeless youth seeking services in several shelters and nonresidential programs in New York City over an 18-month period. Similar studies have been conducted in Los Angeles in an area of Hollywood where homeless youth gather (Robertson, 1989) and at a health clinic which serves many "street youth" (Yates et al., 1988). These studies and specific data from additional urban sites provide the best information about the type of youth who comprise shelter seekers in New York City, the sample used in this study.

DEMOGRAPHICS

The age of runaway and homeless youth is generally defined as between 12 to 17; however, those who have turned 18 may have identical profiles. Most reports find the majority of these youth are 15 years old or older (Council of Community Services, 1984; Robertson, 1989; General Accounting Office [GAO], 1989). The ethnicity of these youth reflects the ethnic breakdown of the local geographic community (GAO, 1989). In fact, most runaway and homeless youth come from their local community (Chelimsky, 1982; Rotheram-Borus and Bradley, 1991; Shaffer and Caton, 1984; Robertson, 1989; Rothman, 1985). Thus, while the majority of homeless youth nationally are white (70%) and do not receive public assistance (GAO, 1989), samples in

New York City are predominately African-American and hispanic (80-90%) and from poor families (Shaffer and Caton, 1984; Rotheram-Borus and Bradley, 1991).

FAMILY PROBLEMS

Family conflict and serious communications problems tend to be the common theme reported as causing homelessness among youth (GAO, 1989). The severity and nature of conflicts vary greatly. Sexual orientation, sexual activity, pregnancy, school, rejection by a stepparent, and alcohol and drug use are commonly reported sources of conflict (DeMan et al, 1993: DeMan et al 1994; Post and Douglas, 1994;Chicago Coalition, 1985; Robertson, 1989; Rothman, 1985). Family disruptions such as divorce or separation often related to parental alcohol or substance abuse are commonly reported (Rothman, 1985). Shaffer and Caton (1984) found that more than half have parents who are alcoholics, substance abusers, or convicted criminals. Parental alcohol abuse has been consistently found related to runaway behavior (Van Houten and Golembiewski, 1978) and homelessness among adolescents (Miller et al., 1980; New York State Council on Children and Families, 1984; National Network, 1985; Rothman and David, 1985).

Histories of neglect, physical abuse and sexual abuse are reported in all samples, although rates vary depending on the site and method of data collection (Janus, 1995; Warren and Moorhead, 1994; Kufelt and Nimo, 1987; Kurtz et al., 1991). In one national study involving 17 shelters, staff estimated that 5% or less of their clients had been sexually abused (Chelimsky, 1982). In Los Angeles, service providers estimate that 26% of their clients have been sexually abused (Rothman and David, 1985), and a study in Toronto reported that 38.2% of runaway boys had been sexually abused (Janus et al., 1987).

Estimates of physical abuse also vary greatly (Warren and Moorhead, 1994; Barden, 1990; Bucy, 1990; Hermann, 1988; Rothman and David, 1985). Robertson (1989) reports that 37% of runaways suffer physical abuse. Shaffer and Caton (1984) report that more than half of their sample were physically abused by a parent. Farber et al. (1984) found that a sample of runaway youth showed little difference in their description of abusive family histories from a sample of youth who were identified as abused by the state child protective agency.

Given the troubled family histories of most runaway and homeless youth, it might be expected that social supports from parents and guardians would be nonexistent or unsatisfactory. In fact, maintaining contact with families may be a source of added stress rather than the expected source of assistance. Certainly, given the stresses and the multiple problems experienced by runaway and homeless youth in their family settings, it is not surprising that their lives are filled with instability, changes in living situations, and multiple episodes of homelessness.

RESIDENTIAL INSTABILITY

Homelessness among youth appears to be part of a long pattern of residential instability. For many youth it appears more the outcome of a process than a single event (Stefanidis et al, 1992; Institute of Medicine, 1988; Miller et al., 1980). Runaways and homeless youth consistently report family disruptions and extensive separations and moves (Robertson, 1989). Contact with social service agencies and institutional placements are frequent (Solarz, 1986).

Many of these youth have been in foster homes and in other residential settings repeatedly, beginning at an early age (Kashubeck et al, 1994; New York Council, 1984; Rothman, 1985). Shaffer and Caton (1984) found that half of the 118 youth interviewed in runaway and homeless youth shelters had spent some time in the foster care system. More than 20% had most recently resided in an institutional setting. The Greater Boston study (1985) found that most of the residents of 11 youth shelters in Massachusetts reported contact with state and private agencies. Many left home before the age of 13 (57%) and reported continual residential instability. In Hollywood, 40.9% of a "street" sample reported having been in foster care at least once, 38.2% reported been in a group homes, and 56% in juvenile detention (Robertson, 1989). "Like all system kids, their lives are spent traveling through the limbo of foster care, psychiatric hospitals, emergency shelters, residential schools, and the streets" (Greater Boston Report, 1985, p. 7).

There also appears to be a direct relationship between institutional care and homelessness. Youth leaving institutional settings or foster care often become homeless due to poor discharge planning and follow-up (Institute of Medicine, 1988; Solarz et al., 1986). In a New

York City study, 823 minors were found discharged to their "own responsibility" in 1982 (Citizens Committee, 1983). One-third of a sample from Hollywood reported that they became homeless after separation from their most recent placement or detention (Robertson, 1989). Due to a lack of appropriate placements, youth who are in foster care may be returned to prior living situations that were dysfunctional or victimizing. "The lack of available out-of-home resources (e.g. foster and group homes) is more influential in service planning than the needs of the adolescents and their families" (Greater Boston Report, 1985, p. 7).

The impact of changing, unstable living situations on these youth has not been directly studied. However, studies of the effects of unstable and changing placements in foster care on child and adolescent adjustment can shed some light on the potential importance of residential instability as a factor in adjustment and problem behaviors. Research on the number of foster care placements has demonstrated a significant relationship between the number of placements and length of time in foster care and the presence of behavioral or emotional problems (Fanshel and Shinn, 1978; Olsen, 1982; Pardeck, 1982; Runyan and Gould, 1985). Runyan and Gould (1985), for example, found that there was a significant correlation between the number of foster home placements and convictions for criminal activity among foster children and that risk for delinquency increased dramatically with each additional foster placement.

Many developmental researchers and theoreticians in child welfare have cited the detrimental effects of lack of permanency for children and the negative consequences of drifting in foster care. Goldstein, Freud, and Solnit (1973), in influential work on foster care, elaborated on the kinds of problems which can result from a child being removed from a significant other. Shireman emphasizes that children in foster care have difficulty forming a positive sense of self when separated from parents and not settled into a home of their "own," and that damage is done to children's ability to learn and trust in new relationships when continuity of care is not provided (Shireman, 1983). Fanshel and Shinn's 1978 study of children in foster care concluded that children not adopted or living with their own families come to think of themselves as unwanted.

Proch and Taber (1987) describe the pattern of alienation among adolescents in foster care, and Zimmerman (1988), in applying the learned helplessness theory of Seligman to children in foster care, presents two ways of understanding the importance of unstable placements in foster care. Proch and Tabler (1987) point out that disruption in foster care placements results from children and caregivers struggling for control, a struggle that becomes more salient at adolescence. They note that for many youth a pattern of instability in placements begins at adolescence as youth begin to experiment with adult roles and behaviors. Indeed, once a pattern of disrupted placement begins, placements tend to be shorter as the adolescent becomes more alienated, expecting rejection. A battle for control results in greater and greater disruption and increased alienation and behavioral consequences for youth.

Zimmerman (1988) uses Seligman's theory of learned helplessness to explain the prevalence of depression and "depressive behavioral equivalents" such as behaviors related to conduct disorder, among children in foster care. Zimmerman points to family environment as well as the experience in foster care as factors in causing children to feel that they have no control over their lives. Many children from difficult home environments view themselves as responsible for the trouble at home and feel unable to produce any positive outcomes. Repeated changes in living situation confirm their feelings of being unable to control events or of only causing negative events. Repeated placements and changes in living situations are, from this perspective, "depressogenic" and contribute to children's maladjustment and problem behaviors.

Clearly, residential instability is a factor in homelessness among youth. Research evidence indicates that changes in living situation and repeated movement through foster care placements can adversely affect youth's development. It is likely that residential instability would have a strong relationship to adjustment and behavior problems among runaway and homeless youth. Understanding the impact on youth's development of repeatedly running away or being thrown away and/or of being repeatedly placed is a key focus of this study. That is, does residential instability show a direct relationship with adjustment and problem behaviors in this population? Does it increase homelessness and concomitant adjustment and behavior problems indirectly through reducing social supports or by directly increasing maladjustment and problem behaviors that will result in homelessness?

ADJUSTMENT AND PROBLEM BEHAVIORS

Studies have consistently found that runaway and homeless youth in urban samples have significant problems in adjustment with high rates of depression, low self-esteem, conduct problems, alcohol and drug abuse, and suicidality. In addition, recent studies have confirmed high rates of sexual risk taking and prostitution which places these youth at risk for HIV infection. There has been a desire among service providers and policy makers to avoid labeling homeless youth on the basis of behavior and feelings that occur during survival on the streets. However, there is growing evidence that many chronic problems appear in this population. In fact, a consensus exists in the runaway service community that the population has become more troubled in recent years (Rothman and David, 1985).

Rates of DSMIIIR disorders including major depression, conduct disorder, and post-traumatic stress, were found at least three times higher among homeless youth in Hollywood when compared to a non-homeless population (Mundy et al, 1990). Runaway and homeless youth in a New York City sample were found to have psychiatric profiles indistinguishable from adolescents attending a psychiatric clinic (Shaffer and Caton, 1984). These researchers concluded that much of the psychiatric disturbance was present before the current runaway or homeless episode. Evidence of specific adjustment and behavior problems is reviewed to confirm the high rates found in previous studies.

Depression

Research has consistently found high rates of depression and histories of suicide attempts among runaways. In Los Angeles, Yates, et al. (1988) found that 83.6% of the youth were depressed at a rate more than three times that of a comparable sample of non-runaway youth. More than 18% of these adolescents had a history of attempting suicide.   In a recent study of youth in runaway shelters in the southeastern U.S., Kurtz, Jarvis, and Kurtz (1991) found 38% of their sample to be depressed. Estimates using diagnostic criteria for depressive disorder ranged from 26% (Robertson, 1989) to 71% (Shaffer and Caton, 1984). Mundy et al. (1990) discovered that homeless youth in Los Angeles show above average number of symptoms for dysphoria and are significantly more depressed than a normative sample.

Rates of past suicide attempts were found to be as high as 49% in a sample from Hollywood California (Robertson, 1989) and to be close to one-third among youth in shelters in New York City: Rotheram-Borus and Bradley (1990) report 27% boys and 33% girls; Shaffer and Caton (1984) report 15% boys and 33% girls. Robertson (1989) reports that 29% of homeless youth had made a suicide attempt in the past year, while Rotheram-Borus (1989) found that more than 10% of the sample had made attempts in the month previous to entering the shelter.

Self-esteem

Data on the self-esteem of runaway and homeless youth are quite limited and those which do exist do not present clear results. Several have described low rates of self-esteem among runaway and homeless youth (Janus, Burgess, and McCormick, 1987; Englander, 1984; Kurtz et al., 1991). For example, Englander (1984) found significantly lower social self-esteem among female runaways when compared to non-runaways. They are more likely to attribute socially undesirable traits to themselves than are non-runaway girls. However, Sher (1991) reports in the National Canadian Youth Study that homeless youth report high levels of self-esteem, comparable to levels reported by college students and same-age peers living at home. Adams et al. (1985) describe a mixed picture regarding runaways' self-esteem. While more than 80% of their sample felt they were persons of worth, almost four out of five felt that they were failures with more than 60% reporting that they were not proud of themselves and 605 saying they felt useless. Samsa, Masten, and Ramirez (1990) report that adolescents living in homeless shelters for families have a more negative self-image than adolescents living at home. Many runaway youth view themselves as needing help. For example, Post and McCoard (1994) found that runaways feel that they are not good family members and have dissapointed their families. Shaffer and Caton (1984) report that 38% percent of New York runaways see themselves as needing help for emotional problems.

Conduct Problems

Conduct problems including truancy, fighting, stealing have been found to be extremely high in the runaway and homeless youth population. Shaffer and Caton found that 60% of runaway and homeless youth meet diagnostic criteria for conduct disorder. Price (1987) reports that more than half have been expelled or suspended from school. Of those enrolled in school, a substantial number have conduct disorders (GAO, 1989). One in three runaways in southeastern U.S. shelters reported unruly behavior in school to be a problem (Kurtz et al., 1991). As a result of behavior and learning problems, one-quarter of runaways in Los Angeles had repeated at least one grade and another quarter were placed in special education classes (Robertson, 1989). Many runaway and homeless youth have had problems with the criminal justice system. Robertson (1989) reports that 56% have spent some time in a detention facility. In New York, one-quarter of the girls and half of the boys have been arrested or put in jail (Shaffer and Caton, 1984). DeMar et al (1994) report finding runaway behavior associated with vandalism, theft, and overt delinquency.

Many of the behaviors which are typically used to evaluate conduct problems appear to be part of a runaway's strategy for surviving homelessness. Many youth report breaking into buildings for a place to sleep (Yates, 1988). Between 10% and 30% report trading sex for food or shelter (Rotheram-Borus, 1989; Robertson, 1989). In a literature review, the American Medical Association (1986) concluded that one out of three homeless males engage in prostitution. Robertson (1989) found that about half of runaways report having sold drugs for money. However, many youth who report various problem behaviors do so only when they are homeless (Robertson, 1989).

Substance Abuse

High rates of substance abuse have been reported among runaway and homeless youth. Yates et al. (1988) found that more than 80% of homeless youth in an outpatient clinic reported drug use. In a survey of runaway service providers it was reported that an estimated half of the youth were abusing drugs (Rothman and David, 1985) while in New York City 70% of a shelter sample reported some drug use (Shaffer and Caton, 1984). Koopman et al (1994) report that 46% of a shelter sample use drugs, with most of users reporting use of more than once a week. Alcohol use also appears prevalent among runaways, with rates reported as high as 60% using regularly (van Houten and Golembriewski, 1978). Rates of alcohol abuse in studies in Los Angeles are reported to be about 50% (Robertson, 1989; Yates et al. 1988) and were 71% in a New York City sample (Koopman et al, 1994). IV drug use appears to vary greatly. It was found to be 7% in Houston (Hudson, 1989) and 3 to 7% in New York City (Shaffer and Caton, 1984) but 35% among homeless youth at an outpatient clinic in Los Angeles.

Robertson et al. (1988) in their extensive study of drug and alcohol use among homeless adolescents in Hollywood found that almost half met criteria for a diagnosis of alcohol abuse or dependency at some point in their lives. Fully two-thirds of those with diagnoses of alcohol abuse or dependency also met the criteria for a diagnosis of drug abuse. These researchers used an inner city health clinic for comparison with a population of adolescents who might be considered high risk but not homeless, and found that homeless youth were nine times more likely to have a diagnosis of substance abuse.

It is unclear how much of the substance abuse predates runaway episodes and residential instability. However, it is likely that for many youth drug abuse problems, like other adjustment and behavior problems, may be exacerbated by time on the streets or in changing living situations.

Sexual Risk Taking

Sexual risk behaviors are more common among runaways than youth who do not runaway. Pregnancy and teen motherhood is more common among homeless youth than non-homeless populations (American Medical Association Council on Scientific Affairs, 1989; Miller and Lin, 1988; Price, 1987). Shaffer and Caton (1984) found 36% of their sample were pregnant and that those who had been abused were less likely to use birth control. Robertson (1989) found that half of the runaway girls reported that they were pregnant. Runaway and homeless youth start having sexual intercourse at an average age of 12.5, which is a significantly earlier age than other adolescents (Yates et al., 1988; Rotheram-Borus, 1989; Zelnick and Shah, 1983). Condom use has been found to be inconsistent among homeless youth (Hudson et al., 1989; Rotheram- Borus, Rosario, and Koopman, 1991) and between 50% and 71% of street youth have sexually transmitted diseases (Shalwitz, 1990).

The rates of HIV infection found among runaway populations further demonstrates the high frequency of sex risk behaviors among this population. Existing data on seroprevalence indicate that about 4% of homeless youth, or 60,000 individuals, are infected. The rates vary from city to city with 2.1% in Houston and 5.3% in New York City. Seropositivity among this population is two to ten times higher than those found in youth in the Job Corps (St. Louis et al., 1989). A recent national study (Allen et al, 1994) found 10.8% of a runaway sample had known HIV risk exposure with seroprevalence rates varying among different sites.

STRESS

The most common strategy for evaluating stress has been through measures of stressful life events. These events are viewed as a possible precipitating factors in the onset of symptomatology in both health and mental health. The effects of such events (e.g. financial problems, changing jobs, divorce) are thought to be additive. Holmes and Rahe (1967), who pioneered work in this area, focused on the adaptive behavior required to adjust to events and developed an index of life stress based on common life events in adult samples.

Since the initial development of life events measures, several areas of evolving theory, research, and debate have developed which are germaine to this study. First has been the application of stress theory and life events to adolescents and the integration of developmental theory into the creation of life events variables. Second, and related, has been the growing evidence that all change is not equal in creating stress and that events can have different meanings to individuals. A third important development is the increasing recognition that measures of stressful events and their relationship to adjustment may reflect more chronic stress or "strain" in certain populations.

Adolescence is described as a period in which dramatic transitions and changes occur and a time during which life long competencies and coping styles emerge. Research on the effects of stress during adolescence has been conducted over the past decade although it lags behind such research with adult populations. Compass et al. (1986) points to only ten studies which examined the "association of cumulative life events with psychological and/or physical dysfunction among adolescents" (p.206). In these studies a range of life events measures were used and few of these studies investigated factors that might mediate the relationship between life events adjustment and problem behaviors. In addition, Compass (1987) states that the measures of dysfunction were idiosyncratic and nonstandardized.

Despite the limitations of the research on adolescent stress, there has been general agreement on the types of items that should constitute a life events scale for teenagers. These stress measures have focused on clusters of events relating to school, peers, sexuality, health, family, deviance, relocation, and distress. Furthermore, there has been consistent evidence in studies that certain stressful life events have an impact on health and mental health in adolescents (Johnson and McCutcheon, 1980; Gad and Johnson, 1980; Hotaling et al., 1978; Hudgens, 1974; Newcomb et al., 1981; Compass et al., 1986). Since the introduction of the Schedule of Recent Experience by Holmes and Rahe (1967) recognition of the importance of separately assessing desirable and undesirable events (Mechanic, 1975; Sarason, Monchaux, and Hunt, 1975) has dramatically increased. Instruments have emerged which seek individualized ratings of desirability and impact. The evidence that desirable and undesirable events are differentially related to dependent health and mental health variables is mounting (Mullis et al, 1993; Sarason, Johnson and Siegel, 1978; Johnson and McCutcheon, 1980; Wenet, 1979).

In studies of adolescents, negative life events have been correlated to psychological symptoms (Gad and Johnson, 1980; Johnson and McCutcheon, 1980; Newcomb et al., 1981; Compass et al., 1986). Yet, impact scores in which participants rated the degree of positive or negative impact of events have been found to add little to the general ratings of positivity or negativity (Johnson and McCutcheon, 1980; Newcomb et al., 1981). However, Johnson and McCutcheon (1980), in agreement with Rahe (1974), suggest that weighting events and differentiating the impact of events may prove of greater significance with "people who have experienced many changes of a major sort" (p. 122).

In research on stress there has been growing recognition that "life events" as measures of discrete experiences do not alone account for differences in susceptibility to disease and maladjustment (Hinkle, 1974; Dohrenwrend and Dohrenwrend, 1969; Gersten et al., 1977;

Pearlin et al., 1981). Dohrenwrend and Dohrenwrend (1969) raise the possibility that the degree of disturbance may relate to pre-existing differences in behavioral pathology rather than stressful events. Differences in pathology may arise as a result of sociocultural factors which have been consistently found to relate to psychological disorder. One's experience in the world and the degree of chronic problems and/or stress may determine the way in which one responds to life events or life crises.

Gersten, Langner, Eisenberg, and Simcha-Fagan (1977) theorize that certain aspects of the life situation generate stress and can be conceptualized as ongoing stressful processes. These processes are of a longer duration in contrast to the change induced stress introduced by the stressful event. As an example these researchers ask, "Is disturbance a function of being continually exposed to lower socioeconomic status or an unhappy marriage plus intervening life-event changes which may occur? Or do the ongoing processes themselves mainly account for later disturbance?" (p. 229). Pearlin, Lieberman, Menaghan, and Mullan (1981) use the concepts of stressful events and life strains to suggest that life events interact with ongoing problems or strains to create distress. They postulate that "life events ... lead to stress by adversely altering the meaning of persistent life strains" or "that life events may create new strains that eventuate stress" (p. 339).

The understanding that stress can not be measured solely by discrete recent life events or by looking for clusters of life events is critical in conceptualizing the nature of stress in a population which has had common ongoing stressors. While this stressor may be only one factor in the complex sociocultural experience of a cohort, it may serve as a measure of an ongoing stress or strain which affects the distress of the specific cohort. Furthermore, it may partially determine the potency of life-events measures in influencing psychological adjustment.

In a sample of runaways, residential instability can be viewed as ongoing stress as well as a series of specific events and could prove a critical determinant of distress. Changes of living situation, runaway episodes, and resulting adjustments and re-adjustments would appear to be a critical source of stress for this population. In fact, a recent survey of runaway needs found that less stress and a better living situation were among the most frequently identified needs by youth themselves (Post and Mcoard, 1994). One would expect that residential stability as a source of stress would have a complex but meaningful relationship with adjustment measures such as depression and conduct problems. For example, does residential instability relate to adjustment directly? Does it affect the meaning of specific recent life events on adjustment? As a stress measure and possibly a measure of unstable relationships, does it have a direct affect on social supports, and do social supports in any way mediate its affect on adjustment?

SOCIAL SUPPORTS

In the 1970s, works by Caplan (1974), Cassel (1976), and Cobb (1976) alerted sociologists and psychologists to the importance of social supports. Since this work, there has been an impressive accumulation of studies which support the relationship of social supports to physical illness and psychological disorder. The most frequently theorized and studied relationship of social supports to health and mental health has been as a buffer to stressful events (Cobb, 1976; Dean and Lin, 1977; Lin et al., 1979; Cohen and Hoberman, 1983). This phenomenon has been found in situations involving problems such as depression, cancer, pregnancy, birth complications, child maltreatment and unemployment (Aneshensel et al., 1982; Berkman and Syme, 1979; Dignam, Barrera, and West, 1986; Broadhead et al., 1983; Gore, 1978; Mitchell and Hodson, 1983; Barrera, 1981; Jorgenson, King and Torrey, 1980). The existence of a buffering effect is a primary focus of this study.

A major weakness of the literature in social supports has been the lack of a consistent conceptual underpinning and the varying definitions and measures used to explore the importance of this broad concept. Vaux and Harrison (1985) state:

> Unfortunately research has often been conducted without the prerequisite theoretical and conceptual analysis of the social support construct, resulting in a plethora of idiosyncratic measures (often post hoc) exhibiting dubious relevance to unclear concepts. Definition-like statements are quite numerous in the support literature, but very few constitute the basis of a theoretical construct. Such statements often combine and confuse references to social ties, interactions, and subjective ties, and the terms social support, social system, and social network are used interchangeably. (p. 246)

Recent conceptual papers have begun to disentangle the components of social supports and there appears to be an increasing consensus that the size, the nature of support interactions, and the perceived satisfaction of supports each represent separable and often independent aspects of social supports (Barrera, 1986; Vaux and Harrison, 1985; Barrera and Ainlay, 1983). Vaux, Reidel, and Stewart (1987) state, "Social supports may be best understood as a meta-construct, referring to three subsidiary constructs: social network resources; supportive behaviors; and subjective appraisals of support" (p. 209). Barrera (1986) differentiates social embeddedness which includes social network measures such as size, density and multiplexity; perceived social support which includes measures of availability and adequacy; and enacted support, measures which "compliment the other measures by assessing what individuals actually do when they provide support" (p. 417).

Although providing different paradigms, Vaux and his colleagues (1985) and Barrera (1986) emphasize the probability that specific measures of social supports will prove prognostic of specific adjustment or behavior outcomes. The challenge is to define clearly the aspects of social supports under study. Researchers need to evaluate whether specific components of social supports are related most to specific dependent measures of health or mental health.

Selection of social supports measures for this study emerged from a review of literature on adolescent social supports and networks and on social influences on adjustment and problem behaviors. Although this literature reflects the lack of consistent definitions, two primary areas of interest emerged. First, what components of social supports appear to influence adolescent adjustment and problem behaviors? Second, what does literature on social supports indicate about parent and peer influence on adolescent adjustment? Studies of social supports and the adjustment and problem behaviors of adolescents have primarily focused on social supports' buffering effect on stress. The results have been equivocal, and there are substantial differences in sample populations and measures of both supports, and adjustment and behavior problems. In a study of the relationships of younger adolescents, Condry and Siman (1974) report that inadequate parental support was associated with a greater peer orientation, and peer orientation predicted socially undesirable values and more frequent reports of undesirable behaviors (meanness to peers, disobedience to adults).

Sandler (1980) studied whether the presence of three resources of social supports (i.e. one vs. two parents; the presence of older siblings; and ethnic congruence in the community) moderated the effects of stress on poor children. Parental and sibling support factors were found to be associated with lower levels of maladjustment. Ethnic congruence was not. It is noteworthy that Sandler focused on the presence or absence of a support person rather than support specific activities or perceptions of social supports. Nevertheless, this work provides evidence that specific sources of support, particularly parents and family, can influence adjustment.

Burke and Weir (1978) explored differences in the relationships among stress, social supports, and physical and emotional well-being in adolescent males and females. This research team compared two sources of support, parents and peers, using limited measures of social interactions and satisfaction. They found that there were gender differences in the choice of parent versus peer support. Females were more likely to use peer supports and yet were found to have a greater degree of stress and poorer physical and emotional well-being than males. The potentially negative effect of specific sources of support emerged in this study.

Gad and Johnson (1980) investigated the relationship among social support, race, socioeconomic status, degree of life stress, and adjustment. While finding higher levels of stress and maladjustment in poor adolescents, independent of race, Gad and Johnson (1980) found no evidence that social supports played a significant mediating role between stress and adjustment. However, these researchers did not differentiate between sources of support and they used as a social supports variable total ratings of perceived support without differentiating various sources or support activities. The lack of specificity of their support measure may have resulted in finding no significant results.

Cauce, Felner, and Primavera (1982) studied the structure of social supports and their relationship to adjustment among adolescents from "high stress lower socioeconomic class inner- city backgrounds" (p. 429). They used a measure of perceived helpfulness or support in examining the relationship between three sources of support (i.e. family, formal, and informal) and academic adjustment and self concept. This study confirmed that the effect of support on adjustment was found to vary greatly, depending on the source as well as the adolescent's gender (and perhaps ethnic background). For example, family support was found to be associated with better scholastic self concept except among African American females, where it was associated with poorer scholastic self-concept. Adolescents with higher levels of informal supports (e.g. from peers) showed significantly poorer academic adjustment but higher peer related self-concept.

Vondra and Garbarino (1988) investigated the importance of social supports in the development of social competence and behavior problems among adolescents. They included measures of perceived support (satisfaction) and network size and content while focusing on the importance of parents and kin in predicting the dependent variables. Among teenagers aged 14 to 16 years, parental support was significantly related to social competence and a greater percentage of kin in the network predicted fewer behavioral problems. In fact, a proportionately greater inclusion of peers or adults outside the family was associated with behavior problems among the more "troubled" youth in this study.

The research on adolescent social supports is consistent with theories of social development. Both indicate the continued importance of parent and family relationships and the increasing influence and, for some, the negative effect of peer relationships during adolescence. When the sources of social supports are specified, the presence of parents and kin in the network and/or perceived support from parents were most consistently linked to adjustment or well-being. The significance of support from peers was unclear and often appeared negative. This finding raises the need to include more information on peer values, norms, or behaviors in assessing peer influence. In addition, the direct relationships between stress and adjustment and problem behaviors, and those between stress and support proved stronger and more consistent than the buffering effect of social supports.

There is additional evidence in literature on child maltreatment and drug use and from clinical practice that the existence of stable relationships with parents or other related adults may decrease maladjustment and problem behaviors (Rubin et al, 1992; Rohner and Rohner, 1980; Burgess, Anderson, and Schellenbach, 1988; Jessor and Jessor, 1975; Burke and Weir, 1978). At the same time, there is clear evidence from research on problem behaviors and substance abuse that peer and friend behaviors can increase risk (Hawkins and Fraser, 1984; Huba et al., 1980; Braucht et al., 1973; Gorsuch and Butler, 1976; Kandel, Kessler, and Margulies, 1978).

While most studies with adults and adolescent samples have found that perceived satisfaction is most often significant in buffering stress and affecting adjustment, there is reason to focus on social support size and content variables with a population of mostly poor, unstable adolescents. Such youth have been found to present high levels of support with little variability (Gad and Johnson, 1980) possibly indicating a need to fantasize support or reflecting low expectations of having support needs met. McGowan and Kohn (1990) found that poor pregnant teenagers had few available social supports and expressed little need for various types of supports and generally high satisfaction. Rotheram-Borus (1991) found in a review of social supports among a sample of runaway youth that runaways who appear to have the least support claim the most satisfaction and expressed the least need. She suggests that these youth have been so consistently lacking social support that even in confidential interviews they show no recognition of the value of social supports. Because unstable, often emotionally neglected runaways appear to offer little variability in perceived satisfaction, it may be the network variables such as size, number of peers, inclusion of parents, which relate to adjustment.

Because of the inconsistent influence of peers, this study includes an assessment of perceived norms and behaviors related to substance abuse and to sex behavior within social support networks. The availability of information about the dangers of these risk behaviors within the social network will also be evaluated. For the runaway populations whose supports can often be from "the street," these may prove critical social support network variables in predicting high risk behavior.

III
Methodology

LOGIC OF THE APPROACH

This study has an exploratory design which utilizes quantitative descriptive data related to runaway and homeless youth to test basic hypotheses and to better understand key characteristics of this population. Four key variables are described: *residential instability, acute stress, social supports, and adjustment and behavior problems.* The relationships among these variables are explored through a path analysis as demonstrated in Figure 1. These findings are described in Chapter 4.

Residential instability is used in this study as an index which represents a measure of a type of chronic stress. Constantly changing living situations and the insecurity of placements with families or institutions is shared by many runaway and homeless youth. The development of specific indicators of residential instability related to runaway history and residential history was a key part of the study. Residential instability is hypothesized as relating to adjustment and behavior problems and, as a stress variable, to be mediated by social supports.

Acute stress is measured by stressful life events and is hypothesized to be affected by runaway youth's experience of the type of chronic stress measured by residential instability. In addition, acute stress is viewed as being buffered by social supports.

In choosing social support network variables to use in this study, several factors were important. First, it was critical to use an instrument which had enough face validity to provide interesting and potentially useful information in its specific questions. Second, it was decided, due to time considerations and to lack of conceptual clarity in the field, not to explore the emotional content of relationships and the subjects' perceptions of individual supportive interactions. In addition, this approach was consistent with the challenge of looking at the types of activity and experience of the runaway youth without assessing the complex emotional experience of these youth.

Third, an understanding of adolescent development, social learning, and the development of specific problem behaviors led to the addition of questions about the behavior of social network members. Substance abuse and sexual behaviors among network members, and especially peers, might play a critical role in determining the ways in which social supports influence related behaviors and adjustment. The large and "satisfactory" social network of a runaway youth can consist of crack dealers, prostitutes, and other street people, with no well-adjusted peers or parental figures included. In a preliminary way, this aspect of social support networks is explored in this study.

Finally, variables for adjustment and problem behaviors had to be selected which represented meaningful areas of concern for runaway and homeless adolescents and which were not overly confounded by the experience of running away. For example, problems such as fighting with siblings or truancy might be viewed as substantial indicators of behavior problems in certain samples of youth. In the runaway and homeless population, these behaviors may primarily result from running away and, taken alone, not be meaningful indicators of adjustment or behavior problems. The variables chosen are depression and self-esteem for adjustment and conduct problems, drug use and sexual risk taking for problem behaviors. These variables were thought to be meaningful indicators of adjustment and problem behaviors, and also to provide variables which could be used to assess the existence of an underlying problem behavior syndrome (Jessor and Jessor, 1978).

RELATIONSHIP TO THE LARGER STUDY

This study is part of a larger research project, AIDS Prevention Among Adolescents with High Risk Behaviors, part of the HIV Center for Clinical and Behavioral Studies located at New York State Psychiatric Institute and funded by the National Institute for Mental Health. The primary goal of the AIDS Prevention study is to develop and evaluate an intervention strategy for two adolescent populations considered at high risk for contracting HIV infection: runaway and homeless youth and homosexual male youth. Three community programs have been used for data collection and for the implementation of an AIDS intervention model. Two are runaway shelters which are funded by Federal and State runaway and homeless youth grants. The third is a multiservice agency for gay and lesbian youth which includes a range of nonresidential services included individual and group counseling, educational services, and a drop in center.

As the initial Project Director of the AIDS Prevention Among Adolescents with High Risk Behaviors Project, the author was involved in developing instruments, coordinating with community agencies, and hiring and supervising staff. Because of the author's interest in working on this smaller study, he became primarily responsible for the selection of instruments to be used to measure social supports and life events, and the creation of variables related to instability. Although the author left his role as project director in the fall of 1988, he continued to consult for the study and contribute to the exploration and interpretation of findings. The author has received consultation in completing the analysis of this study from the data analysis staff of the AIDS Prevention Among Adolescents with High Risk Behaviors Project.

The AIDS Prevention Among Adolescents with High Risk Behaviors study included a comprehensive baseline interview, a series of group and individual interventions on site and follow up interviews at 3, 6, 12, 18, and 24 months in order to assess behavior change in the subjects receiving intervention. This larger study was conducted over a five-year period and included 150 runaway youth who received the intervention, 150 runaway youth in the control group (who received current practice related to HIV risk prevention), and 150 gay youth who received the intervention.

The current study was taken from the baseline interviews conducted at the two runaway and homeless youth sites. Data from the first 130 youth receiving the baseline interview are included in this study. These interviews were conducted over a six-month period at both the intervention and control shelter sites.

DATA COLLECTION

The baseline interviews were conducted with new clients within two days of intake, after the initial treatment plans and orientation had been completed by agency staff. Interviews were conducted by research assistants who were assigned to the shelters and who had become familiar with each program and were seen by staff and youth as a part of the overall program. These interviewers, employed by the AIDS Risk Prevention Among Adolescents Project at New York State Psychiatric Institute, received extensive training in conducting research related interviews as well as consistent supervision from the author and from the principal investigator.

The baseline interview, which took approximately two hours, was generally conducted in two sessions. It contains numerous components evaluating such areas as sex attitudes and behaviors, history, problem solving skills, ethnicity, and socio-economic status as well as the stability, social supports, and adjustment variables used in this study. Youth were paid $5 to participate; and if they completed the baseline and participated in intervention activities, they were paid $20 for each follow-up interview that occurred at 3- and 6-month intervals for 2 years. There were two refusals to participate out of initial the 130 youth. A few adolescents were discharged or left the shelter programs before the interview could be completed.

KEY CONCEPTS AND OPERATIONAL DEFINITIONS

RUNAWAY YOUTH: Youth away from home or legal guardian more than 24 hours.

Operational Definition: Youth receiving residential services in one of two runaway shelters.

RECENT STRESS: State created by the interaction of a person with social and environmental demands (stressors). "Stressor" can be used to indicate environmental noxious stimulus and "stress state" to indicate the consequences of such exposure (Cassel, 1974). Life changes or events which necessitate adjustment are sources of "stressors" and contribute to a "stress state."

Operational Definition: Number of negatively experienced stressful life events on the Life Events checklist (Johnson and McCutcheon, 1980) to which specific runaway and gay items have been added.

CHRONIC STRESS: State of strain generated by ongoing disturbances, pressures, and/or changes. Life events which become chronic or continuous in nature can create a state of chronic stress as can continuous economic hardship or long-term volatile relationships.

Operational Definition: Residential instability as an indicator of an ongoing change and disturbance for the runaway sample is considered a measure of a type chronic stress. Specific measures used to develop the residential instability variable are defined below.

RESIDENTIAL INSTABILITY: The degree to which an adolescent has remained consistently in home settings and/or with guardians. This is not viewed as an assessment of relationships but of stability in terms of living situations. As a measure of changes in living situation over time, residential instability is actually a measure of chronic stress.

Operational Definition: Set of scores including age of first running away, number of runaway episodes, and number of types of different living situations. The following two stability related variables were factored from these scores.

1. Runaway history consists of the number of runaway episodes, age of first running away, and homeless vs. not homeless (youth's perception that s/he had no home or considered the shelter as home).

2. Placement history consists of the number of types of living situations (including various types of placement, family settings, and street), length of time since a youth was last in a stable living situation (of more than 3 months), and whether a youth has ever lived in an institution.

SOCIAL SUPPORTS: Resources available to an individual through other people or groups of people. These resources can include, for example, material aid, emotional support, advice, social activities. It is, in fact, an overly broad concept, a meta-construct referring to subsidiary constructs (Vaux, Riedel, and Stewart, 1987). Three theorized constructs are social embeddedness, perceived social support, and enacted social support, each of which is derived from asking about the social support exchanges and the characteristics of the individual's social support network (Barrera, 1986).

Operational Definition: The Arizona Social Support Interview Schedule (ASSIS) (Barrera, 1981) is used to gather information about the three key constructs of social support.

1. *Social Embeddedness*: "The connections that individuals have to significant others in their social environments" (Barrera, 1986, p. 415).

    Operational Definition: Social Embeddeness is characterized by the total number of persons in an individual's support network when a subject is asked to list who provides specific social support exchanges i.e. intimate interaction, physical assistance, social participation, and informational support. Embeddedness measures used in this study include the total number of persons in the network, the presence of parents or other related adults in the network, the number of peers in the network, and the number of people using drugs or alcohol in the network.

2. *Enacted Supports:* An assessment of what individuals actually do when they provide support, of the helping behaviors which constitute the provision of support resources.

    Operational Definition: A measure of the frequency of types of support exchanges which have been actually carried out as well those which are perceived as available. It is evaluated by asking about specific support exchanges in the past month. Youth are asked who they went to for intimate interaction, physical assistance, and social participation.

3. *Perceived social supports*:   The cognitive appraisal of being reliably and adequately connected with others, that is, the perceived adequacy and availability of support.

    Operational Definition: Perceived support in this study is limited to scores of perceived need for and satisfaction with types of support exchanges, i.e. intimate interaction, physical assistance, and social participation. In addition, global need and satisfaction scores are calculated using the means of support exchange scores.

ADJUSTMENT: Adaptation to psychosocial stressors present during development. Maladaptive reactions can impair social, educational or occupational functioning.
Operational Definition: Two variables, depression and self-esteem are used to evaluate adjustment.

1. *Depression*: Evidence of a clinical syndrome symptomized by dysphoric mood, loss of interest and pleasure, loss of energy, as well as other specific behaviors and feelings.
   Operational Definition: Score using depression subscale of the SCL-90 (Derogatis et al., 1976).
2. *Self Esteem*: Self evaluations related to positive or negative values placed on one's own attributes
   Operational Definition: Scores on the Rosenberg Self-Esteem Scale (Rosenberg, 1965).

PROBLEM BEHAVIORS: "Behavior that is socially defined as a problem, a source of concern, or as undesirable by the norms of conventional society ... and its occurrence usually elicits some kind of social control response" (Jessor and Jessor, 1977, p. 33). These behaviors indicate a lack of adjustment and have been empirically and experientially shown to increase risk of further health and mental health difficulties.
Operational Definition: Problem behaviors are measured using three distinct scores based on runaway and homeless youth's behaviors.

1. *Conduct problems*: repetitive and persistent patterns in which the basic rights of others or major age appropriate rules or societal norms are violated.
   Operational Definition: Score on Assessment of Conduct Problems (Rotheram-Borus and Bradley, 1990; Rotheram-Borus, Rosario, and Koopman, 1991), a scale derived from the diagnostic DSMIIIR criteria for conduct disorder.
2. *Drug use*: Use of illegal substances or abuse of legal drugs or medications.

Operational Definition: Frequency of drug use in the past 3 months.

3. *Sexual risk taking*: Sexual behavior which places one at risk for HIV infection or other sexually transmitted diseases.

Operational Definition: Score on the Sexual Risk Behavior Assessment Schedule for Youth (Meyer-Bahlberg et al.,1988), a four-point risk scale based on the number of sex partners, the number of sex episodes, and the frequency of condom use for those having intercourse.

STUDY SITES

The data for this study are derived from the initial 130 baseline interviews at the two runaway shelter sites. These two programs are Project Enter Runaway Shelter located in East Harlem in Manhattan and Urban Strategies Runaway Shelter located in the Bushwick section of Brooklyn. Each shelter has 20 beds and receives funding through the New York State Runaway and Homeless Youth Act. Both are in New York City and serve youth between the ages of 12 and 17 years old. Although each is located in a distinct community, neither has a catchment area and both serve youth from throughout New York City, as well as from other cities and states.

The shelters, Enter and Urban Strategies, are funded to provide emergency shelter for runaway and homeless youth and to develop plans and referrals within 30 days of intake. However, funding sources frequently grant permission for shelters to extend specific adolescents' care for weeks and occasionally months. Both Enter and Urban Strategies receive referrals from many sources, such as human service agencies, schools, police, other youth, and runaway hotlines. Services are voluntary and nonsecure so that only teenagers who wish to stay remain at the shelter. Adolescents who break specific rules regarding behavior, particularly related to substance abuse, sexual contact between clients, or violent behavior may be referred elsewhere or discharged from care. There were two refusals for participation in the study and about 15 adolescents left the shelters or were discharged before a baseline interview could be conducted.

The youth who seek services in the shelters are mostly from New York City although there is a small group who come from other parts of New York state or out of state. The youth in both sites are mostly African-American and hispanic, with a small population of white adolescents. There are no significant differences between the sites in terms of age, ethnicity, referral source, or problems at intake (Rotheram-Borus, Rosario, and Koopman, 1991). Thus the data collected at the two shelters is combined for the purpose of analysis. Based on a previous study of 576 consecutive runaway youth entering shelters in New York City (Rotheram-Borus and Bradley, 1991) it was anticipated that the population would be nearly equally male and female, have a mean age of about 15.5, and be about 60% African-American, 25% hispanic, and 15% white, Asian or interracial.

In addition to providing shelter for runaway and homeless youth who come directly from the street, these programs also provide temporary, emergency placement for youth referred from the Human Resources Administration, Child Welfare Administration or from specific voluntary institutions needing a place to shelter an adolescent. These youth, known as "system kids" (Bucy, 1989), usually have open cases in the Child Welfare Administration (CWA), New York City's child welfare agency and have usually been in placements or have been closely monitored at home. They are sent to runaway shelters when there is no immediately available placement which is appropriate for them, often being referred from the emergency placement office after a crisis. They may have been removed from home after an apparent episode of parental abuse or have had extreme problems in a family court ordered placement. Approximately 30 "system kids" were included in the 128 youth in the study.

INSTRUMENTATION

The data for this study are taken from six parts of the baseline interview. The first part of the baseline interview assesses demographic characteristics, runaway history and residential history (Appendix A). The second part explores recent life stress (Appendix B). Part three gathers information about current social supports (Appendix C). It focuses on size, nature, and satisfaction with supports while also exploring the perceived amount of substance abuse in the social support network. The last three parts evaluate current adjustment and problem behaviors. Included in these are depression (Appendix D), self-esteem (Appendix E), and conduct problems including drug abuse (Appendix F) and sexual risk taking (Appendix G).

DEVELOPMENT OF INSTRUMENTS AND PILOTING

The development of the baseline interview involved a series of steps to ensure the validity and reliability of each of its components. First, focus groups were held with youth in runaway shelters to determine the best way to conduct the baseline interviews and to ask about key factors which contribute to homelessness and should be assessed if one was to understand the causes and consequences of being homeless. These groups focused on logistical issues such as when and where to do the interviews; how to involve interviewers on site so they could best establish trust in a population of adolescents who were anticipated to be distrustful; and how long an interview could be done at one time. Focus groups also focused on youth's relationships with family, with peers, types of behaviors which were typical on "the street," and particularly on attitudes and behavior related to risk related to sex and drugs.

In addition to talking to runaway youth, staff in runaway shelters were interviewed in order to take advantage of the clinical and experiential knowledge of social workers and paraprofessionals who work with runaway and homeless youth. Chart reviews were also conducted to determine priority areas for the baseline interview.

After each component of the interview was drafted it was piloted and reviewed in several ways. First, staff in the shelters reviewed the instruments to give feedback about content and about youth's ability to comprehend the instructions and questions contained in each component. Then each component was field tested with a small group of runaway and homeless youth, after which a focus group was run to obtain feedback about the content and about the specific questions. Components of the baseline were drafted and revised several times based on information received through piloting and focus groups. As an example, stress questions related to being victimized and related to sexual orientation were added after focus groups. Questions about the substance abuse of specific individuals listed as providing social supports were eliminated and replaced by a general question about the number who use drugs when it was evident that youth were uncomfortable sharing this information even under strictly confidential circumstances.

To check the reliability of demographic characteristics and history obtained in the interviews, chart reviews were done to compare consistency of the information given to interviewers with that given to intake workers in the shelters. For all other baseline components, including life events, social supports, and adjustment and problem behavior related instruments, test-retests were done with small samples of youth over a two week period. This piloting activity revealed high reliability in youth's responses throughout the baseline interview.

Demographics And Home History

The key demographics aside from age, sex, race, and ethnicity, all relate to current and past stability. While there are limitations imposed by the primary interests of the broader research project, several questions are used to assess degree of stability and the youth's perception of their current status. The key variables assessed in this section and the specific questions used to develop each variable follow:

Homeless vs. Not Homeless

Where do you think of as home right now?
1. Has no home
2. With parents
3. With mother
4. With other relative
5. With friends
6. With foster family
7. In group setting (e.g. group home)
8. At this shelter
9. Other (specify)

Number of runaway episodes

1. How many times have you run away or left home? By running away or leaving home I mean at the time you left home you did not plan on coming back, and you stayed away at least overnight without your parents' permission or without their knowing where you were? (If youth was thrown away, proceed to b.)

2. Have there been times that you were forced or asked to
    leave by your parents/guardians? If yes, how many time
    did this happen?
    a.   one time
    b.   two times
    c.   three times
    d.   four times
    e.   five or more times

Age of first running away (or being thrown away)

How old were you when you first did that (ran away) or were
thrown out?
1.   Under 12 years old
2.   12 years old
3.   13 years old
4.   14 years old
5.   15 years old
6.   16 years old
7.   17 years old
8.   18 years old

Time of last continuous 3 months with parent or guardian

When was the last time you lived with a parent or a guardian
for more than 3 months?
1.   Within the last week
2.   Two weeks to a month ago
3.   Between 1 and 2 months
4.   Between 2 and 6 months
5.   Over 6 months ago

Number of types of living situations

I'd like to ask you about places that you have lived.
1.   With a foster family placed by a social worker
2.   In a group home
3.   In a foster care institution (residential treatment center)
4.   In a mental hospital
5.   In a detention center
6.   In a work camp or prison
7.   On the streets
8.   At the home of a teenage friend
9.   Independently--alone or on your own

10. At the home of a relative (not including your parent or legal guardian)
11. At the home of an adult friend

Institutional Experience

This variable was created by combining responses given to the question about previous living situations. All who had lived in any of the following were considered to have had institutional experience:

1. Group home
2. Foster care institution
3. Mental hospital
4. Work camp or prison

These variables can be used to gain a picture of past stability and current status, as well as the adolescent's perception of his or her status. They were used to create variables related to residential stability or chronic stress.

Social Supports

The social supports instrument is a variation of the Arizona Social Support Interview Schedule (ASSIS) developed by Barrera (1981). The ASSIS was designed to examine the characteristics of "available" and "actual" networks and to provide information concerning individuals' subjective appraisal of the adequacy of supports. It measures network size and content in terms of who is available and who has been actually used in support activities in the past month. The ASSIS interview contains six categories of social support: intimate interaction, physical assistance, positive social interaction, advice, material aid, and positive feedback. Network members who are available and those to whom one has gone for this category of support are listed for each category. The age, sex, and type of relationship of each network member is noted allowing the beginning understanding of who individuals go to for what type of support activities.

In addition, perceived need for each category of support as well as perceived satisfaction with supports received in each category (intimate, physical, advice, social, material, and positive feedback) is scaled. Subjects are asked to rate their satisfaction with the supports they received and to rate how much they needed those supports during the past month. Need scores are derived from a 5-point scale and satisfaction from a 7-point scale (see Appendix C). Combined need and satisfaction scores can be derived by calculating the mean of each of the scores across all six categories of support.

The ASSIS provides information about social embeddedness, that is, the size of adolescents' available and actual network as well as some understanding of social enactment, that is what social activities look like and with whom. It does not explore the social conflicts, emotional and behavioral content variables of relationships or perceived support by key support network members. It reveals whether adolescents use peers, family, or other adults to get social needs met and to whom they turn for such social activities as advice or feedback.

Reliability of the ASSIS was assessed by Barrera (1987) using test-retest of 45 undergraduate students at least 2 days apart. Total network size, that is the number of people providing at least one support function, had a test-retest reliability of .88, and 73.8% of those network members mentioned in either the test or the retest were named in both. The support satisfaction showed a moderate test-retest correlation of .69 and low internal consistency (coefficient alpha = .33). The support need demonstrated a good test-retest correlation of .80 and moderate internal consistency (coefficient alpha = .52). Barrera (1987) determined correlations of network size between the ASSIS and the ISSB, an earlier assessment instrument aimed at different aspects of social supports, in order to establish the ASSIS's validity. A correlation of .32, $p<.05$, was found between the ISSB and network size.

Several changes and additions were made to the ASSIS for this study. First, material aid and physical assistance were combined into a single category. Many social support researchers do not distinguish these categories (Brim, 1974; Hirsch, 1980; Pattison, 1977; Tolsdorf, 1976). Barrera (Barrera and Ainlay, 1983) noted difficulty in a factor analysis of drawing a distinction between these two categories. In addition, pilot interviews with 20 runaway adolescents revealed almost no difference in the responses in these two categories in terms of need, satisfaction, or content variables.

Following the initial 20 pilot interviews it was decided to use three categories of social support in the study: intimate interaction, physical assistance/material aid, and socializing interaction. Because of the interest of the study in high risk sex and drug related behaviors in the AIDS Risk Study, the advice activity was divided into specific categories related to information and advice about drug and alcohol and about sex. In addition, the subjects' perception of substance abuse and sexual activity among the social support network members listed was explored. Social support questions were asked orally and scored using a grid, hand cards, and an additional scoring sheet. The primary social support network variables selected for use in the study are listed and described in the following:

1. *Social embeddedness* for intimate interactions, physical assistance, and socializing interactions. This was assessed by the number of persons listed in response to the following questions:

   a. (Intimate) If you wanted to talk to someone about things that are very personal and private, or if a situation came up where you needed some advice, who would you talk to?

   b. (Physical Assistance) Who are the people who would give up some of their time and energy to help you--things like drive you someplace you needed to go, helping you do some work around the house, going to the store for you, things like that?

   c. (Social Participation) Who are the people you get together with to have fun or to relax?

   Youth are instructed to list all the people who they would name (or initial) as a response to these questions, and are specifically told to list individuals more than once if appropriate and to think carefully about whether there are more people who might be considered.

2. *Social Enactment* for intimate interaction, physical assistance, and for social participation. These are assessed by asking the following questions:

   a. (Intimate interaction) During the last 3 months, which of these people did you actually talk to about things that were personal and private, and which people gave you advice?

   b. (Physical Assistance) During the last 3 months, which of these people actually pitched in to help you do things that you needed some help with?

   c. During the last 3 months, which of these people did you actually get together with to have fun and relax?

3. *Satisfaction* with intimate interaction, physical assistance, and social participation is assessed by asking how satisfied or dissatisfied the interviewee was with each type of support given. Each of the three satisfaction scores was chosen from a hand card listing the following seven choice responses:
    a. Very dissatisfied
    b. Moderately dissatisfied
    c. Slightly dissatisfied
    d. Neither satisfied or dissatisfied
    e. Slightly satisfied
    f. Moderately satisfied
    g. Very satisfied

4. *Need* for intimate interaction, physical assistance, and social participation is assessed by asking how much the interviewee thought s/he needed each type of support during the past 3 months. Each of the three need scores was chosen from a hand card listing the following five choice responses:
    a. No need at all
    b. Slight need
    c. Moderate need
    d. Great need
    e. Very great need

5. *Total network size* is the sum of all individuals listed in the network.

6. *The inclusion of parents or guardians* as providers of supports and

7. *The number of peers* in the network are created from the relationships which youth attribute to each person listed in the network. These variables are created after the list of support persons is completed. For each person given as providing any type of support, the youth is asked: What is this person's relationship to you?

    The type of relationship is coded. If a youth lists a father/stepfather/male guardian or mother/stepmother/female guardian, a parent or guardian is considered to be included in the network. The number of peers listed in each youth's support network is summed to create the score for number of peers.

8. *Drug use in the network.* To assess this variable youth were asked after completing the list of providers of support: Of the people you've mentioned so far, how many do you think or know use drugs?

In order to obtain information about the norms of the social support network several additional questions were asked about the knowledge, attitudes, and behaviors of the people listed in the network.

Recent Stressful Events

Johnson and McCutcheon who have developed and tested the Life Events Checklist (1980) which forms the basis of the instrument used in this study, report the distinct effects of desirable and undesirable events. The evidence that desirable and undesirable events are differentially related to dependent health and mental health variables is mounting (Sarason, Johnson and Siegel, 1978; Johnson and McCutcheon, 1980; Wenet, 1979). In an adolescent population experiencing high rates of negative life events, it is these which are expected to be correlated with high risk behaviors.

The Life Events Checklist (LEC) contains positive and negative ratings for each event and an impact score. Johnson and McCutcheon (1980), in agreement with Holmes and Rahe (1974), thought it might prove of significance with people who have experienced many changes of a major sort. Based on piloting with runaway adolescents it was decided to alter the instrument to combine positive and negative ratings with a simplified impact score. Youth were thus asked to indicate whether an event was very bad, somewhat bad, somewhat good, or very good. An additional change from the LEC involves the time frame. Rather than cover events in the last year, it was decided to ask about stress in the past 3 months. This was based on two reasons: first, the relative instability and high stress of the population and, second, the 3-month follow-up interview schedule of the AIDS Prevention Study.

Piloting with the runaway sample also led to the addition of 16 items to the 46 contained in the LEC. These items emerged out of focus groups with runaway adolescents who had completed and reviewed the LEC. See Appendix 1 for the complete instrument with added items noted. Two types of items were added. The first group reflect the inner city experience of these youth and their unstable lifestyle. The following items of this type were added:

- Changed residences more than twice
- Expelled from school
- Physically assaulted
- Raped/sexually assaulted
- Robbed/burglarized
- Arrested but not convicted of a crime
- Convicted of a crime
- Parent's substance abuse
- Friend's substance abuse

Additional items were added which were to be answered by gay identified adolescents. Given estimates that up to 1 out of 3 youth in shelters are gay or lesbian teens, the following items which attempted to assess stress related to sexual identity were added:

- parents discovered that you are gay
- family members other than parents discovered you are gay
- came out regarding sexual preference to parents
- came out regarding sexual preference to sibling
- came out regarding sexual preference to friends
- friends discovered that you are gay or bisexual
- had someone ridicule you for your sexual identity

Clearly an instrument that did not cover major sources of stress would not be valid. However, given the number of changes which were made to the basic LEC items, a substantially different instrument has emerged.

Depression

Depression is assessed using subscales of the SCL-90 Self Report Symptom Inventory, a 90-item multi-dimensional self-report aimed at measuring symptomatic behavior and distress. It is designed as both a screening instrument and as a measure of symptom status. The SCL-90 provides information about the following nine symptom dimensions: somatization, obsessive- compulsive behavior, interpersonal sensitivity, depression, anxiety, hostility, phobic anxiety, paranoid ideation, and psychoticism (Derogatis, 1977). The depression dimension was established and validated in the context of the Hopkins Symptom Checklist, an earlier instrument from which the SCL-90 evolved

(Derogatis et al., 1973). The developers of the SCL-90 (Derogatis et al., 1976) briefly describe the symptom construct defined by the depression dimension as follows:

> Depression - Reflects a broad range of concomitants of the clinical depressive syndrome. Symptoms of dysphoric affect and mood are represented as signs of withdrawal of interest in life events, lack of motivation, and loss of vital energy. The dimension mirrors feelings of hopelessness and futility as well as other cognitive and somatic correlates of depression. Several items are included concerning thoughts of death and suicidal ideation (p. 321).

Numerous studies have validated the use of the SCL-90 to measure depression and the other symptom dimensions (Derogatis et al., 1976). In a study of construct validity (Derogatis and Cleary, 1977), all nine symptom constructs showed at least moderate levels of theoretical-empirical agreement. Derogatis and Cleary (1977), using measures of factorial invariance, found agreement between males and females on the respective definitions of the symptom constructs. The SCL-90 thus appears established as reliable across the variable of gender. The SCL-90 has been used extensively with adolescent populations (Friedman and Clickman, 1987; Kandel and Davies, 1982; Shaffer et al., 1988; Kashani et al., 1989). The depression subscale has been used as a measure of depressive symptomatology in numerous studies over the last 20 years (Derogatis, 1990).

A factor analysis was conducted to determine the inclusion of specific items in a final score of depression. The results of this analysis and of a Cronbach's Alpha for reliability are presented in Chapter 4.

Self-Esteem

Self-Esteem is measured with the Rosenberg Self-Esteem Scale (Rosenberg, 1965), a 10-item Guttman scale. It is a measure of global self-evaluation rather than a measure of specific facets of self-evaluation. Several studies have demonstrated that one factor underlies the Self-Esteem Scale (Hensley, 1977; and Simpson and Royal, 1975). It was developed and field tested with white and African-American adolescents and is currently the most popular instrument used to evaluate self-esteem in both adolescent and adult populations (Blasovich and Tomaka, 1991). The Self-Esteem Scale has a

Coefficient of of 92% and a Coefficient of Scalability of 72% (Rosenberg, 1979).

Many researchers have established the reliability and validity of the Self-Esteem Scale. Dobson et al. (1979) report a Cronbach Alpha of .77 and Fleming and Courtney (1984) obtained a Cronbach Alpha of .88 for their sample. Fleming and Courtney (1984) also reported a test-retest correlation of .82 for 259 male and female subjects with a one-week interval. Silber and Tippett (1965) reported a test-retest correlation of .85 after a two-week interval with a small coed sample. Numerous researchers have demonstrated that the Self-Esteem Scale is associated with self concept characteristics such as popularity (Lorr and Wunderlich, 1986), academic self concept (Reynolds, 1988), and social confidence (Fleming and Courtney, 1984), as well as other measures of self-esteem (Demo, 1985).

The 10 items that make up the Self-Esteem Scale require that the respondent choose from four responses (strongly agree, agree, disagree, strongly disagree). Responses are scored 1 through 4, with resulting scores ranging from 10 to 40. The Self-Esteem Scale was self-administered by participants in the study.

Conduct Problems

The instrument used for assessment of conduct problems was developed for use with high risk adolescent and field tested with runaway youth (Rotheram-Borus and Bradley, 1991; Rotheram-Borus, Rosario, and Coopman, 1991). It is based on 15 items taken from behaviors listed in the Diagnostic and Statistical Manual of Mental Disorders (DSMIIIR) as criteria for conduct disorder. Although aimed at evaluating conduct problems, this scale is not a diagnostic tool. Two additional items, one related to trouble with family prior to running away and the other related to gang activity, have been added. Thus, the instrument has 17 items. The complete instrument is located in Appendix 1. Youth are asked how many times in the past 6 months they have engaged in one of the 17 behaviors. Answers are given on a 5-point scale with the following response range:

1. 5 or more
2. 3 to 4
3. 1 to 2
4. Not at all

The resulting score is continuous and can be used to determine the relative degree of problem behavior. A factor analysis was conducted to determine the inclusion of specific items in a final score of conduct problems. The results of this analysis and of a Cronbach's Alpha for reliability are presented in Chapter 4.

Drug Use

Drug use was measured by asking participating youth about frequency of use of any drugs during the past 3 months (contained on Conduct Problems Scale in Appendix F). The score used for this study is based on scaled responses to frequency and, while not attempting to give a thorough picture of substance abuse, is intended to provide a brief measure of individual's drug use. Youth are asked how often in the past 3 months they have used drugs. The scaled responses are:

    1.   5 or more
    2.   3 to 4
    3.   1 to 2
    4.   Not at all

Sex Risk Behavior

High risk sex behaviors are assessed using items drawn from the Sexual Risk Behavior Assessment Schedule Youth (SERBAS-Y) (Meyer-Bahlberg, Ehrhardt, Exner, and Gruen, 1988). This semi-structured interview elicits information on psychosexual milestones, lifetime sexual activities, condom use, screening of partners, sexual and sensuous activity in the past 3 months, use of drugs and alcohol in sexual encounters, contraception, and erotic fantasies. All of these issues, except contraception and erotic fantasies (see Appendix G), are explored separately for opposite-sex and same-sex partners. The majority of items inquire about frequency or provide a forced-choice format.

The SERBAS-Y was developed and revised during the initial phase of the AIDS Prevention Among Youth with High Risk Behaviors Project. Piloting was done with runaway youth of both sexes as well as focus groups to ensure that items were understood and that the instrument was thorough in assessing the adolescents' range of sexual experiences. Specific versions of the SERBAS-Y were developed for females, for heterosexual males, and for homosexual males, the primary target groups for the AIDS Prevention study. The variables related to sexual behavior that are used in this study are aimed at assessing current sexual risk.

The specific items used to assess sexual risk taking emerge from questions about sexual activity in the past 3 months. These items are abstinence or nonabstinence, the number of partners, the number of sex occasions (intercourse), and the frequency of condom use. It should be noted that in this study the concept of sexual risk taking related to risk for HIV infection and sexually transmitted diseases and not to pregnancy. Given the current concern about AIDS, it has become critical to view sexual promiscuity and pregnancy prevention within an AIDS prevention context. Thus other methods of birth control are not included in risk assessment. From the above items two 5-point risk status scales regarding sexual risk in the past 3 months were created:

Risk Status 1
   0   Sexually abstinent
   1   Frequent condom use and 1-10 occasions
   2   Frequent condom use and over 10 occasions
   3   Infrequent condom use and 1-10 occasions
   4   Infrequent condom use and over 10 occasions

Risk Status 2
   0   Sexually abstinent
   1   Frequent condom use and 1-2 partners
   2   Frequent condom use and 3+ partners
   3   Infrequent condom use and 1-2 partners
   4   Infrequent condom use and 3+ partners

After an analysis of these two scales was conducted to determine the relationship between the scales, it was evident that the scales were highly correlated and provided little variation in the assignment of risk status to individual youth. Risk Status 1 was chosen for use in this study and is to measure sexual risk taking in the data analysis.

DATA ANALYSIS

The data analysis for this study had several stages. Based on the uniqueness of the sample and the lack of previous research which utilizes many of the specific concepts and variables created for this study, it was critical to explore the empirical nature of the measures of residential instability and to establish the validity and usefulness of the measures with this population. These measures could be used to determine the significance of relationships between the key variables: residential instability; social supports; stressful life events; and adjustment and problem behaviors.

The first step in the analysis was to explore the residential instability variables, to construct indices of each construct in order to reduce the number of variables, and to determine the degree to which the disparate variables represent underlying measures of instability. This was done through manipulating the hard data and through a factor analysis of the six primary measures of residential instability.

The second step in the analysis was to explore the social support measures that emerged from the ASSIS instrument (Barrera, 1981) in order to decide which indices of social embeddedness, perceived social supports, and social enactment would be included in further analysis. While most of these decisions were made based on pre-existing hypotheses, the selection of several measures was based on reviewing the reliability and the trends apparent in the responses of this unique runaway sample. For example, the selection of whether to use an aggregate satisfaction score for satisfaction with social supports or to use only a specific measure, such as satisfaction with intimate support, was based on observation of the initial base rates as well as the results of correlation matrices of specific social support measures.

The third step in the analysis was to review the adjustment measures used in this study. A factor analysis determined the reliability of the depression and conduct problem scales with this population. Base rates for specific measures of adjustment were compared with those found in previous studies to determine the validity of data and the generalizability of findings about the runaway sample in this study.

A fourth step in the analysis was to determine the extent to which gender, ethnicity, and age influenced the key variables. Ethnic differences in measures of residential instability, stressful life events, social supports, and adjustment and problem behaviors were examined between African-American and hispanic adolescents. The other ethnic groups, including White, were extremely small in number. No significant ethnic differences exist in measures of residential instability, stressful life events, social supports or adjustment and behavior problems. Gender was also found to have no significance on most key variables. However, gender did relate to depression and conduct problem scores, findings consistent with research on adolescent adjustment and problem behaviors (Leslie, 1974; Kandel and Davies, 1982; Jessor and Jessor, 1977).

Because the range of age for the sample is quite narrow (14 and 17 years), there was little expectation that age would be a meaningful factor. Only behavior which reflects adolescent developmental tasks such as sex risk activity, and behaviors which increase over time (e.g. the number of runaway episodes) vary significantly by age. These findings are discussed in Chapter 4.

To explore the relationships between the primary variables of interest in this study--residential instability, stressful life events, social supports, and adjustment and behavior problems--a series of Pearson product moment correlations were conducted. After determining the existence of significant findings and examining trends which emerged from these correlations, a regression analysis was used to examine the relative effectiveness, as well as the direct and indirect effects of residential instability, stressful life events, and social supports on adjustment and problem behaviors.

DEFINING THE SAMPLE

The sample of youth who have participated in this study reflect the demographics of all of the adolescents who seek shelter in these two agencies. Of 129 runaways and homeless youth included in the study, 64 were males and 65 females. Although the percentage of males and females varied in each shelter over time, there was a fairly even number of boys and girls seeking shelter. The average age of the boys is 15.9 and the girls 15.7 with an SD of 1.5. The sample is 63% African-American, 26% hispanic, 7% biracial, and 4% white or Asian. Less than 10% of the sample come from outside New York state, with more than 90% from New York City. In terms of religion, 42% described themselves as Catholic, 40% as Protestant, 4% as Muslim, 4% other, and 10% as having no religion.

In the sample only 34% are in school full time with another 8% in school part time. Twenty percent have full-time work and 15.5 % work part time. Forty-five percent receive money from family for support and another 34% receive assistance from adult friends. Although one would assume an underestimate of youth who admit to supporting themselves through illegal means, 12.4% said they obtained money through dealing drugs, 2.3% through prostitution, and 3.9% through other illegal activities. However, when data on problem behaviors and sex risk taking are examined in Chapter 4, it is apparent more youth have been engaged in these activities than report so directly.

It is important to acknowledge that these youth are not representative of runaway and homeless youth throughout the nation. In fact, these youth likely have more in common with teenagers in trouble in New York City than they do with runaway youth from suburban or rural areas. These youth are primarily African-American and hispanic from the inner city; many have had multiple episodes of running away or having been thrown out of home or placements. Many have been in placement and many have experienced continuing instability in terms of living situation during their childhood and teenage years. However, the experience of instability and of high stress which characterizes these youth make them an important group in which to explore the degree to which residential instability, stressful events and social support variables influence adjustment and problem behaviors.

VARIATION IN THE SAMPLE

There is some variation in the sample size for different variables. There were sections of the baseline interview, primarily those which were self-administered, which were not completed or were completed unreliably by youth. This resulted in missing data in specific areas or study domains. No substantive difference in outcomes results from the variability of sample size.

RUNAWAYS AND "SYSTEM KIDS"

Using Bucy's definitions of runaway status (Bucy, 1989), 73% of the sample are current runaways while 27% are "system kids" who needed emergency placements and who have been placed in shelters by child welfare workers. This substantial subgroup is surprisingly large and growing, clearly a major reason for crowded runaway programs and limited beds.

The "system kids" often had difficulty answering questions related to reasons for running away or number of runaway episodes as they have been removed from family by the courts or have been voluntarily placed. They may refuse to answer questions about home expressing that they have not lived at home for years. During the gathering of data for the study, it became apparent that a number of "system kids" were being sheltered. This necessitated looking at this group separately in an initial stage of the analysis in order to make a decision about whether to include this group of teens in the subsequent analysis.

A series of *t*-tests and Pearson correlations were done to determine whether there were differences between the "system kids" and other runaways on key variables. There were no differences in demographic variables of sex, age or ethnicity. Significant differences were also lacking in social support variables and in the outcome measures of depression, conduct problems, or drug use. Based on these findings, the decision was made to combine the two shelter populations in subsequent analyses.

LIMITATIONS

Several important limitations of this study have already been mentioned. First, the sample of runaways represents consecutive intakes in two shelters in New York City and, at best, represents runaway and homeless youth in similar urban settings. Furthermore, the process of self-selection of clients for shelter means that this sample is not clearly representative of all homeless youth. Many do not seek shelter programs and others leave before an intake can be completed.

As part of a larger study, there were time constraints which limited the depth and breadth of questions about residential instability and social support networks. Emotional content of individual interactions and conflictual relationships are not explored in either schedule. Potentially important information about feelings attached to family and stability of living situation as well as feelings of perceived supports needs exploration in further studies.

The study is also limited by its design and analysis. As data are gathered during a single baseline interview, it is impossible to be certain about the direction of relationships which are found and one cannot overstate the predictive value of the findings. However, factor analysis and regression analysis should reveal whether stability and social support networks can provide an avenue by which to understand the problems and needs of runaway and homeless adolescents.

IV
Analysis

Chapter 4 presents descriptive statistics for the runaway sample in four domains: residential instability, stressful life events, social supports, adjustment and problem behaviors. Afterward, the relationships among the variables contained in the four domains is explored. For domains which were developed for this study, it was necessary to construct scales and/or indices and to select a reduced number of scores to use in further analysis. A discussion of the correlations, partial correlations and the results of a regression analysis examining the hypothesized relationships among variables in each domain comprises the second part of the chapter.

DESCRIPTION OF THE VARIABLES IN THE SAMPLE

Residential Instability

Residential instability was assessed with six subcomponents: (a) the age at the first runaway experience; (b) the number of runaway episodes; (c) the number of different living situations; (d) length of time since last at home; (e) homeless or not homeless; and (f) the presence or absence of institutional experience.

Table 1 shows the percentage of males and females giving specific responses to each of the six subcomponent measures used to assess residential instability. More than half of the runaways in the sample have been in an institutional setting at some point in their lives, with no significant difference between the rates for runaways based on gender. Many runaways, 36% of the females and 25% of the males, report that they have no home or consider the runaway shelter to be their home.

The length of time since youth have been at home also did not vary significantly between males and females, with about 25% having been at home in the last week and an additional 21% having been at home in the last 2 weeks. Only 8% report having been away from

TABLE 1

*Indices of Stability of Living Situation. Percentages for
Variables and Mean
Numbers for Number of Homes, Number of Episodes,
and Age at First Running Away*

	Male	Female	Total
Institutional Experience	54.3%	45.7%	53.7%
Homeless	25.0%	35.6%	30.1%
Length of Time Since at Home			
Within Last Week	25.8%	24.6%	25.2%
2 Weeks	19.4%	23.0%	21.1%
1-2 Months	8.1%	6.6%	7.3%
2-6 Months	17.7%	13.1%	15.4%
> 6 Months	29.0%	32.8%	30.9%
Number of Homes	3.2	2.8	3.0 (1.5)
Number of Runaway Episodes	3.4	2.9	3.1 (1.6)

Once = 20%
Twice = 16.7%
Three = 19.2%
Four = 14.1%
Five or more = 29%

Age at First Runaway Episode
(in years)

Less than 12   = 24.0%
12 years   = 14.7%
13 years   = 13.3%
14 years   = 16.7%
15 years   = 14.7%
16 years   = 12.0%
17 years +   = 5.0%

home from 1 to 2 months, although almost 18% report having been away for 2 to 6 months. Nearly 30% have been away from home longer than 6 months. Thus, the majority of runaways in the shelters (55%) report having left home more than 1 month ago.

Runaways have been in an average of three different types of settings and there was no significant gender differences in the number of settings (males, 3.2; females, 2.8). This number specifically reflects the types of living situations which the runaways in this sample have encountered. These numbers do not reflect the number of total changes in living situations since youth's complex histories and poor memories of early experiences made an accurate count difficult.

There is great variability in the number of runaway episodes described and a fairly even distribution between those with one episode and those with five or more episodes. Only 20% of the youth have runaway once; 16.7% twice; 19.2% three times; 14.1% four times; and 29% five or more times. The mean number of episodes of 3.1, standard deviation of 1.6, indicates variability in the number of runaway episodes described by the youth. There is also great variability in the age of youth's first runaway episode with 24% having first runaway at less than 12 years old and more than half by the age of thirteen. There is no significant gender difference in the age of initially running away.

Table 2 shows the break down of responses for different types of living situations and responses for current "home" by gender. The responses reflect the fact that runaway and homeless youth experience numerous living situations and little residential stability. Three specific living situations seem to be experienced by many more males than females in the sample. One quarter of the males have been with a foster family and less than one fifth of the females. Almost one half of the males have been in group home settings, while only slightly more than one third of the females. Although more than 21% of the youth indicate that they had at some time viewed the street as home, this experience is about twice as common for males (28.1%) than for females (15.2%).

There were substantial gender differences in the number of youth who experienced placements related to the criminal justice system. More than 26% of the males have been in a youth detention center and more than 20% have been in a prison or work camp. Approximately 9% of the females have been in youth detention and only 4.5% have been in a prison or work camp. These differences are consistent with those found by others in delinquent and behavior and arrest rates

TABLE 2

Youth experience of different living situations (In Percentage)

	Male	Female	Total
Foster Family	25.0	19.7	22.3
Group Home	48.4	35.0	41.5
Residential Treatment	18.8	13.6	15.4
Psychiatric Hospital	9.4	12.1	10.8
Youth Detention Center	26.6	9.1	17.7
Prison or Work Camp	20.3	4.5	12.3
On the Streets	28.1	15.2	21.3
At the Home of a Teenage Friend	40.6	39.4	39.2
Independently	28.1	18.2	23.1
At Home of Relative not Including Parent	56.3	56.1	56.2
At Home of an Adult Friend	37.5	31.8	34.6

Where do you think of as home right now? (% of responses)

	Male	Female	Total
Have no home	14.8	8.0	11.4
With parents	8.2	6.5	7.3
With mother	32.8	21.0	26.8
With father	3.3	1.6	2.4
With other relative	11.5	19.4	15.4
With friends	--	1.6	0.8
Other (e.g. foster or group)	11.5	11.3	11.4
This shelter	18.0	30.6	24.4

between male and female adolescents (Hawkins et al, 1991). The range of different living situations experienced indicates that the sample has a mix of "system kids", relatively new runaways, chronic runaways who go from placement to placement, and hard core street youth. This variability reflects the variability among runaway and homeless youth.

Youth in the sample were asked where they considered home at the time of intake at the shelter. This question was used to determine if youth considered themselves homeless. As might be expected many youth, 44.3% of the males and 29.1% of the females, considered home to be with parents, with their mother or with their father. Another 15.4% identified the household of another relative as their home. Despite many placements and despite running away, most youth continue to view parents and relatives as providing home. A smaller number, 14.8% of the males and 8% of the females, responded that they had no home. A surprisingly large number of youth, 18% of the males and 30.6% of the females, choose the shelter as home. This response is interpreted as youth perceiving no home to return to at the time of the interview. In support of this interpretation, it should be noted that interviews are done within 48 hours of each youth's arrival at the shelter. Combining the "shelter" and the "no home" responses results in 36% of the sample, 33% of the males and 39% of the females, being considered "homeless" for the purpose of the analysis.

In order to better understand the relationships among the six measures related to residential instability, and in order to determine if these measures could be viewed as representing one or two distinct underlying dimensions, a factor analysis was performed. Table 3 presents the results of the rotated factor matrix. Two factors emerged with an eigenvalue of greater than 1.0 from this analysis: (a) placement history (Factor 1) and (b) runaway history (Factor 2). These factors became key in the remaining analysis.

Factor 1 has an eigenvalue of 1.4 and accounts for 24% of the variance. The factor loading on these variables and the high correlation coefficients among number of living situations, institutional history, and length of time since at home variables with Factor 1 confirm it as a variable representing placement history. Factor 2 has an eigenvalue of 1.0 and accounts for 17% of the variance. The factor loading and the high correlation coefficients among the number of runaway episodes, age of first runaway episode, and homelessness variables with Factor 2 confirm it as a variable representing runaway history. Factors were

TABLE 3

Rotated Factor Matrix of Stability Variables

	Factor 1 Placement History	Factor 2 Runaway History
Number of Homes	0.83	-0.03
Institutional History	0.72	0.05
Length of Time Since Home	0.44	0.01
Number of Runaway Episodes	0.05	0.93
Age at First Runaway Episode	-0.10	-0.33
Homeless	-0.09	0.26
Eigenvalues	1.4	1.0
Percentage of Variance	24%	17%

loaded and individual factor scores were calculated for each youth for placement history and runaway history. For placement history, factor scores range from -3.87 to 3.72 with a mean score of -.137 and standard deviation of 2.3. For runaway history, factor scores range from -3.8 to 2.51 with a standard deviation of 2.51. Thus residential instability is composed of two factors in all further analyses: runaway history and placement history.

Correlations were conducted to determine whether runaway history or placement history relate to gender, ethnicity, or age. Neither correlate with gender or ethnicity. However, age correlates with placement history ($p = .32$, $<.01$) and with runaway history ($p = -.27$, $<.05$). As the number of placements and length of time since at home would naturally increase with age, it is expected that age will relate to placement history. The negative correlation with runaway history is more difficult to interpret, although it appears to reflect that older youth began running away at an older age and are less likely to perceive themselves as homeless than younger youth in the sample.

Stressful Life Events

Current or acute life stress is measured by recent negative life events. A revised version of the Life Events Checklist (Johnson and McCutcheon, 1980) was used to measure acute stress. The percentage responding affirmatively to having experienced each negative stress item on the checklist in the previous 3 months is presented in Table 4. Stressful events are organized into the following sub-categories, based on the type of stressful event: family stress; moving stress; school stress; peer stress; self stress; health stress; and gay/bisexual stress. The Life Events Scores range from 0 to 42. The mean life event score for the sample is 9.7 with a standard deviation of 7.9. There is a great deal of variability in the scores although it is clear from the frequency of stressful life events reported that runaway and homeless youth are under a tremendous amount of stress.

During the past 3 months, nearly half report an increase in arguments between parents and more than half report increased arguments with parents. Many report having parents involved with drugs (nearly 40%) and 30% report a change in parent's financial status in the past 3 months. About one in four report that their parents have

TABLE 4
Percentage of Youths Experiencing
Each Stressor During Past Three Months

	Males N = 52	Females N = 53	Total N = 105
Family Stress			
New step-parent	17	27	22
Increased arguments between parents	32*	65	48
Increased parental absence	30	44	37
Parents separated	28	37	32
Parents divorced	17	23	20
Increased arguments with parent	45	60	52
Changes in parents' financial status	28	33	30
Parent lost job	17*	39	28
Parent having legal trouble	11	19	15
Parent going to jail	17	9	18
Increased trouble with sibling	28	44	36
Sibling left home	17*	40	28
Family member having drug problems	40	39	40
Family member having illness or injury	25	33	29
Family member died	30	44	37

TABLE 4 (continued)

	Males	Females	Total
<u>Move Stress</u>			
Changing to a new school	32*	54	43
Moving to a new home	51*	73	62
Changing residence more than twice	40	39	40
<u>School Stress</u>			
Failing a grade	40	58	49
Failing grades on report card	26*	56	41
Trouble with classmates	34*	50	42
Trouble with teacher	40	44	42
School suspension	36	33	35
School expulsion	23	23	23
Not making an athletic team	21	29	25
<u>Peer Stress</u>			
Breaking up with girlfriend/ boyfriend	36	31	34
Losing a close friend (other than by death)	26	35	30
Close friend's drug problem	30	15	23
Close friend's serious illness or injury	19*	42	30
Close friend's death	11	35	22

TABLE 4 (continued)

	Males	Females	Total
Self Stress			
Losing a job	26	27	26
Trouble with police but not arrested	21	23	22
Arrested but not convicted of crime	17	15	16
Convicted of crime	19	12	16
Jailed	26	17	22
Robbed or burglarized	21	19	20
Physically assaulted	13	21	17
Raped or sexually assaulted	15	27	21
Health Stress			
Having a drug or alcohol problem	13	23	18
Major personal illness or injury	23	37	30
Getting pregnant	N/A	25	N/A
Having an abortion	N/A	21	N/A
Girlfriend getting pregnant	25	N/A	N/A
Girlfriend having an abortion	13	N/A	N/A

* $p < .05$

divorced or separated in recent months and almost one in three report that a family member has had a serious illness or injury.

Stress related to school is also common. More than 4 in 10 report failing grades on report cards, trouble with classmates, and trouble with teachers. More than one in three have been suspended, and nearly one in four have been expelled from school. An additional 43% report changing schools in recent months. Stress related to friends and romantic relationships was also reported frequently. One third of the youth report ending a romantic relationship in the past 3 months, 23% report having a friend with a drug problem and 30% report having a close friend with a serious illness or injury. In fact, almost one in four report the recent death of a close friend.

Stressors related to victimization are reported alarmingly frequently by runaway youth. One in five over all and one in four of the females report having been raped or sexually assaulted in the past 3 months. About one in five also report having been physically assaulted or robbed. In addition to being victimized, many report having been in trouble with the law. One in five report being in trouble with the police but not arrested, one in six being arrested but not convicted of a crime, and one in six, convicted of a crime. More than 20% report having been in jail.

Stressors reported in the areas of health indicate frequent stress related to substance abuse and sexual behavior. About 18% report having a problem with drug or alcohol use. One in four males report getting a girl pregnant and one in four females report getting pregnant themselves in recent months. A major personal illness or injury is reported by 30% of the runaway youth.

In several domains of stress, there are significant differences between runaway males and runaway females. Female runaways more frequently report increases in trouble with siblings, parental job loss, and increases in parental arguing during the previous 3 months. Changes in school and home are significantly more frequent for females as are failing grades and report cards. The greater school problems may reflect the fact that more females in the sample are enrolled in school. Boys are more likely to have reported a friend having a drug problem while girls more often report having a seriously ill friend. Stressful events related to self and to personal health show no significant differences between males and females in the sample.

TABLE 5

Means and Standard Deviations of Social Support Scores

	Can (Persons Listed)	Did (Persons Listed)	Need (Range 1-5)	Satisfaction (Range 1-7)
Intimate Support	2.7 (2.5)	2.0 (2.1)	3.1 (1.2)	5.6 (1.9)
Physical Support	3.0 (3.1)	2.8 (5.7)	3.1 (1.2)	5.9 (1.9)
Socialization Support	4.8 (3.7)	4.0 (3.4)	3.4 (1.4)	6.1 (1.7)
Total of Supports	3.3 (2.7)	2.7 (3.0)	3.4 (1.1)	6.0 (1.4)

Social Supports

Social supports are measured using a variation of the ASSIS Interview (Barrera, 1986), from which several variables were chosen for the initial analysis. Table 5 shows the means and standard deviations of measures of social embeddedness, enacted support, and perceived support derived from this instrument. Social embeddedness is measured by the number of persons who are available for types of support (can) and enacted support by the number of persons who actually offered types of support in the last month (did). Perceived support is measured by two likert scales, one for need for supports and one for satisfaction with supports. Also in Table 5 are total scores for social embeddedness (total can) and enacted support (total did) and perceived support (satisfaction and need), scores based on the mean of three types of support for each social support measure.

From Table 5 it is evident that youth typically report the availability of more than two persons for intimate support, about three persons for physical/material support, and almost five for socializing support. In fact, youth report to have used most of these available supports in the past month as there is little variation between reported can scores and did scores. The standard deviations of these scores ranging from 2.1 for enacted intimate support (did) to 5.7 for enacted physical/material support (did) indicate extreme variability in the number of persons available in the youth's support system.

The measure of need for social supports has a range from one to five, from no need to very great need. The mean need scores for intimate support, physical support, and socialization support are 3.1, 3.1, and 3.4 respectively. These similar need scores can be interpreted as indicating that youth in the sample express moderate need for each type of support. Any expectations that runaway youth would typically indicate either a lack of need or an extreme need for support were not met. The standard deviations of 1.2, 1.2, and 1.4 indicate the range of scores.

The satisfaction with social supports scores range from one to seven, from very dissatisfied to very satisfied. The mean satisfaction scores present a bit clearer picture. The mean scores for satisfaction with intimate support, 5.6, physical support, 5.9, and socializing support, 6.1, all convey moderate to high satisfaction with supports. The standard deviations are relatively less on this 7-point scale, indicating most youth expressed some satisfaction with social supports. Given their histories and current situations, the degree of satisfaction may appear surprising. This finding and others related to the results of social support measures will be discussed in Chapter 5.

To understand the relationships between types of support and to determine the efficacy of using distinct measures of social embeddedness and enacted support for further analysis, correlations were done between can scores for each type of support and total can scores, and between did scores for each type of support and total did scores. Table 6 presents correlations between types of social embeddedness, between types of enacted support, and between types of perceived support. It also shows the correlations between various types of supports and total support scores. There are significant correlations between the number of persons who can provide each type of support ($p<.01$ for all) and significant correlations between each can score and the total can score ($p<.01$). There are also significant correlations between the number of persons who did provide each type of support in the past month except between physical support and socializing support for which the correlation of .16 has a $p = .052$. The correlations between each did score and the total did score is highly significant ($p<.001$). Table 6 demonstrates that the total support scores for both can and did scores represent meaningful indices for use in further analysis.

Table 6 also contains correlations between scores for types of perceived need and perceived satisfaction. These are generally high as only correlations between need for physical support and need for socializing support and between satisfaction with intimate support and satisfaction with socializing support are not significant at $p<.05$. In addition, there are significant correlations between each type of perceived support and total support ($p<.01$). In further analysis, either total need scores and total satisfaction scores can be used to indicate perceived support.

Finally, Table 6 includes correlations between types of support and total network size, that is the total number of different persons given as providing social supports. As expected, social embeddedness (can) and the enacted support (did) scores correlate highly with network size. However, neither perceived satisfaction with supports or need for support shows a significant relationship to network size.

TABLE 6

Correlations Between Types of Enacted Supports and Correlations
Between Types of Perceived Supports

	Intimate	Physical	Social	Total	Network Size
Enacted Support					
CAN					
Intimate	1.0	0.53A	0.25**		
Physical		1.0	0.18**		
Social			1.0		
Total				1.0	
DID					
Intimate	1.0	0.56**	0.21**	0.70A	0.30A
Physical		1.0	0.16	0.88A	0.27A
Social			1.0	0.57A	0.75A
Total				1.0	0.56A
Perceived Support					
NEED					
Intimate	1.0	0.53A	0.25A	0.79A	0.01
Physical		1.0	0.18	0.75A	0.02
Social			1.0	0.71A	0.05
Total				1.0	
SATISFACTION					
Intimate	1.0	0.40A	0.16	0.77A	0.02
Physical		1.0	0.28**	0.78A	0.02
Social			1.0	0.62A	0.08
Total				1.0	

**p< .01   Ap< .001

After reviewing the relationships among measure of support taken from the ASSIS interview, it was clear that there were no consistent patterns emerging which would necessitate using numerous social support measures in further analysis. In fact, total support scores could be used to represent each domain of social support. Based on this preliminary analysis, it was also decided to utilize total social enactment (did) in further analysis and to eliminate social embeddedness (can). Runaway youth generally utilized their available supports each month, as indicated by the similar number of persons who could provide support and those who actually did.

It was also decided to utilize total satisfaction scores to represent perceived support, thus eliminating need for social supports from further analysis. The satisfaction scores showed greater consistency than need scores and represented the area of most interest in assessing youth's perceptions about their social support networks.

For the analysis, several additional social support measures were created to try to assess the nature of runaway youth's support networks more thoroughly. The means scores on these measures for the sample as well as for males and females are presented in Table 7. This table includes the following measures: (a) total network size; (b) the number of peers in the total support network; (c) the number of persons who use drugs; (d) the percentage of youth who included mothers or fathers in their networks; and (e) the percentage who included at least one parent or a guardian in their network.

Gender differences do not appear significant in these variables. The data do not show predominant drug use in these youth's social support networks although it is substantially more frequent in males' networks than females'. About 28% of males' network members use drugs (2.6 persons out of 9.3 total) while about 17% of females' network members use drugs (1.3 persons out of 7.8 total).

The variables presented in Table 7 were included in the initial phases of analysis to explore more thoroughly factors which might contribute to the relationships between instability, social supports and problem behavior. Peers make up approximately the same proportion of network members for males and females with the lower mean for females apparently a reflection of smaller network size. The number of peers in the network and the inclusion of parental figures were viewed as potentially important variables in understanding youth's social supports.

TABLE 7

*Means by Sex for Supplemental Social Support
Measures to Indicate Content of Networks*

	Male	Female	Total
Total Network Size	9.35	7.77	
Number of Peers	5.37	4.29	4.72
Use Drugs	2.63	1.30	1.79
Use Alcohol	3.71	2.00	2.92

*Percentage Included in Runaway Youth Support Networks by
Relationship*

Fathers	23%
Mothers	56%
Siblings	60%
Extended Family	75%
Mother, Father or Parental Figure	66.7%

Adjustment And Problem Behaviors

Adjustment is measured using scores for depression and self-esteem. Problem Behaviors are measured using scores for conduct problems, drug use, and sexual risk taking. The initial analysis of each of these measures differs as the complexity and proven utility of the different measures varies. The following discussion will present initial data which emerged from reviewing each of these dependent variables.

Depression is based on the SCL-90 Scale, which has been used many times with high risk adolescents. Table 8 presents the percentage of responses to individual items on the SCL-90 Depression Scale. The scores range from 0 to 40. The mean score for this sample is 11.9 with a standard deviation of 10.6. A factor analysis resulted in a one factor solution with an eigenvalue of 5.6 accounting for 45% of the variance. Cronbach's alpha for reliability was .87. After converting to Derogatis' Positive Symptom Index for depression (Derogatis, 1976) the runaway sample's mean depression score of .99 is slightly higher than those of .80 found by Derogatis (1983) in a general sample of adolescents. However, the depression scores are much less than those found in inpatient and outpatient adult populations (Derogatis, 1983) and, in themselves, do not appear to indicate significantly high rates of depression among the sample. Girls appear more depressed than boys in the sample ($r = .24$ $p<.01$) a finding consistent with literature comparing depression rates between male and female adolescents (Leslie, 1974; Kandel and Davies, 1982; Teri, 1982).

The Rosenberg Self Esteem Scores are based on a scale ranging from 10 to 40. The mean score for the sample was 30.2 with a standard deviation of 5.6. These scores reveal moderate to high self-esteem among the runaways as a population. Although it is difficult to find a study which utilizes the complete tool and provides generalizable data, it is clear that the fact that the mean scores of the youth in the sample is 75% of the highest possible score makes this a sample whose self-esteem is comparable to that found in other samples (Rosenberg and Rosenberg, 1965; Simmons et al., 1978; Barnes and Farrier, 1985). As with depression, self-esteem, as measured, does not appear affected by the runaways' experience. Self-esteem scores did correlate with age ($r = .1737$ $p<.05$) but not with gender.

The Conduct Problems Scale (Rotheram and Bradley, 1991; Rotheram, Rosario and Koopman, 1991) consists of 16 items, each

TABLE 8

*Percentage of Responses to Individual
Items on the Depression Scale*

During the Past Week, How Much Were Bothered By:

	Not At All	A Little Bit	Moder-ately	Quite a Bit	Valid % Extre-mely
Feeling low in energy	51.0	26.5	4.1	11.6	6.8
Thoughts of ending life	74.7	9.6	2.7	4.8	8.2
Crying easily	53.4	19.2	7.5	9.6	10.3
Feeling of being trapped	63.0	17.8	6.8	4.8	7.5
Blaming yourself	45.0	28.2	10.1	7.8	16.9
Feeling lonely	41.3	23.6	10.8	7.4	16.9
Feeling blue	36.6	33.1	9.0	9.0	12.4
Worrying too much	26.7	25.3	13.3	12.7	17.3
Feeling no interest in things	60.3	21.2	8.2	4.8	5.5
Feeling hopeless	64.7	14.7	5.5	5.5	6.9
Feeling everything an effort	54.8	19.2	8.2	6.2	11.6
Feeling worthless	72.8	14.3	3.4	6.6	3.4

scored from 0 (not at all) to 4 (more than 5 times in the past 3 months). Table 9 shows the percentage of responses for each item on the scale. Scores for the sample range from 12 to 42 with a mean of 18.3 and a standard deviation of 5.99. A factor analysis revealed one rotated factor with an eigenvalue of 30.7 accounting for 21.9 of the variance. Cronbach's Alpha was .83. Conduct disorder did not show a significant relationship with either gender or age.

The Conduct Problems Scale did not attempt to provide a evaluation of conduct disorder among individual youth, and thus is used in analysis to show the degree of problem behaviors reported and to evaluate the frequency of specific items which reflect problem behaviors. Table 9 indicates that about 60% of the sample report skipping school in the past 3 months, with nearly 40% skipping school more than five times. While the degree of truancy may reflect this population's homelessness and residential instability, the percentage of youth who skipped school is likely higher than it appears when runaways who have already dropped out are taken into account. Almost 70% of these youth have been in at least one fight in the past 3 months and 40% have had three or more fights. More than one in four reports using a weapon and almost one in five reports stealing in the past 3 months. The rates of these behaviors reflects a troubled, unstable population, and yet the rates of specific behaviors appears lower than those reported in other runaway and "street" populations (Shaffer and Caton, 1984; Robertson, 1989; and Yates et al., 1988).

Assessment of drug use for the study was developed as a 4-point subscale from the conduct disorder scale. The scale ranged from no use to regular use (more than weekly). Based on previous research with similar populations (Shaffer and Caton, 1984; Rotheram and Bradley, 1991) drug use may be under-reported in the sample. In this study, 32.7% report any drug use with only 21.1% describing regular use. Drug use did correlate highly with gender as males reported significantly more use ($r = .27$ $p<.01$) and also correlated with age ($r = .28$ $p< .01$). Neither finding is surprising as adolescent males have been found to use drugs more than adolescent females (Kandel et al., 1978), and drug use would be expected to increase with age in a sample of young and middle adolescents.

The measure of sexual risk taking is based on a 4-point scale derived from the SEABAS Interview (Meyer-Bahlberg et al., 1988). CON/ACTS is a 5-point scale ranging from abstinence to high risk

TABLE 9

Percentage of Responses to Individual Conduct Disorder Items

In the last three months:				Valid % 5 or
	Not at All	1-2 Times	3-4 Times	More Times
Skipped School	39.4	12.7	8.5	39.4
Destroy Property	84.5	5.6	3.5	6.3
Bully Younger Kids	74.6	7.7	4.9	12.7
Get in Fights	29.6	30.3	12.7	27.5
Use a Weapon	71.8	12.7	4.9	10.6
Lie	46.5	19.7	9.9	23.9
Mug Someone	93.5	3.6	0.7	2.2
Steal	80.1	8.5	0.7	10.6
Set Fires	90.6	5.6	1.4	2.1
Break in (Burgle)	89.4	6.3	2.1	2.1
Forced Sex	98.6	0.7	0.7	0.0
Cruel to Animals	85.6	8.6	2.2	3.6
Use Alcohol	41.8	26.2	10.6	21.3
Use Drugs	68.3	10.6	6.3	14.8
Gang Activity	91.5	2.1	0.7	5.6
Trouble in School	43.7	12.0	12.7	31.7

(numerous sexual acts with no condom use). The runaway sample included 27.4% of the youth who were abstinent. The mean score on the scale was 1.9 with a standard deviation of 1.6. The mean score falls approximately at low/ moderate risk (inconsistent condom use with few acts). However, given the fact that more than one quarter of the sample have a zero score as they are abstinent, there do appear to be many youth with substantial sex risk behavior. As with drug use scores, the CON/ACTS scores correlate with age ($r = .20$ $p<.05$). This relationship reflects the fact that sexual activity emerges and often increases as early adolescents become older.

The problem behaviors assessed in this study are consistent with those which Jessor (Jessor and Jessor, 1977; Donovan and Jessor, 1985) describe as part of a problem behavior "syndrome." To evaluate the degree to which there are relationships between these behaviors in this runaway and homeless youth sample, a correlation matrix was done. The results appear in Table 10. The depression and self-esteem measures are included in the correlation matrix to determine the degree to which adjustment variables correlate with problem behaviors. There is a significant positive correlation between conduct disorder and drug use and between conduct disorder and sex risking taking ($r = .33$ $p<.01$ and $r = .29$ $p<.01$, respectively). However, no significant relationship is seen directly between drug use and sex risk taking.

Depression does not relate significantly with conduct disorder or with drug use but does have a significant negative correlation (-.21 $p<.05$) with sex risk taking behavior. Self-esteem also has no significant relationship with conduct disorder or drug use but does have a significant positive correlation (.16 $p<.05$) with sex risk taking behavior. Apparently greater depression and lower self-esteem decrease risky sex behavior rather than increase it. This puzzling result appears to contradict the assertions that problem behaviors, including sex risk taking and promiscuity, mask depression and poor self image. However, depression and self-esteem do have a strong negative correlation ($r= -.46$ $p<.01$) indicating that runaway youth who are depressed also have lower self-esteem.

To further examine the relationships among these variables, a factor analysis was conducted. The results of this factor analysis are presented in Table 11. Only one factor emerged using the maximum likelihood method with an eigenvalue greater than 1. Depression and self-esteem load on one factor; conduct problems, sexual risk acts, and

TABLE 10

Correlations Among Measures of Adjustment and Risk Behaviors

	Conduct	Depress	Self-Est.	Sex Risk	Drug Use
Conduct Disorder	1.0				
Depression	0.11	1.0			
Self-Esteem	-0.08	-0.46**	1.0		
Sex Risk Behavior	0.29**	0.21**	0.16*	1.0	
Drug Use	0.33**	0.04	0.06	0.11	1.0

* = .05 ** = .01

TABLE 11

Communality of Adjustment and Problem Behavior Measures on Factor 1

	Communality
Depression	0.61
Self Esteem	0.42
Conduct Problems	0.01
Drug Use	0.06
Sex Risk Taking	0.06

Eigenvalue	1.1
Percentage of Variance	22%

TABLE 12

Correlations among measures of social support network, residential instability and life events

	Runaway History	Placement History	Life Events
ocial Enactment (Did)	-0.04	0.05	-0.01
ocial Satisfaction	-0.15	-0.04	0.04
etwork Size	-0.01	-0.12	0.03
arent or Guardian in etwork	0.05	-0.03	0.12
umber of Peers	-0.06	-0.02	-0.08
umber Who Use Drugs	-0.27**	0.10	0.08

* p < .01

substance use were independent factors. Despite the correlations between each risk behavior and conduct disorder, these did not load on one factor. Thus, the theory of a single underlying problem behavior "syndrome" (Jessor and Jessor, 1977) receives little support among runaway and homeless youth.

Relationships Among Domains

Table 12 presents correlations between social support variables and residential instability as well as between social support variables and life events. There are no significant correlations among these variables with the exception of the correlation of -.27 ($p<.01$) between the number of persons in youth's social support networks who use drugs and runaway history. This negative correlation is puzzling as it indicates that runaways with shorter, less lengthy histories of running away have more drug users in their network.

Table 13 presents correlation coefficients of residential instability, life events, and social support variables with adjustment and problem behavior variables. The only significant correlation appears between placement history and drug use (.32 $p<.01$). Youth who have more history of placement in various settings tend to have more drug use.

The hypothesized relationships among residential stability, life events, social support, and adjustment and problem behaviors are outlined in Figure 1. To examine the predictive ability of this model, regression analysis was conducted for each path of this model. Based on the factor analysis, regressions were conducted separately for four dependent variables: adjustment (self-esteem/depression factor), conduct problems, sexual risk acts, and substance use. Residential instability is one independent measure composed of two factors: runaway history and placement history. Social support as an independent measure is composed of two factors: satisfaction and enactment. Stressful events is a single independent measure. Five sets of regressions were conducted on the dependent variables to explore the relationships among residential stability, social supports, and stressful life events.

Table 14 shows the regressions performed to assess the predictive ability of residential stability and the buffering effect of social supports on this variable. First the dependent measure was regressed on residential instability; then the dependent measure was regressed in a

TABLE 13

Correlations between residential instability, life events, social support and adjustment and problem behaviors

	Depression	Self-Esteem	Conduct	Sex	Drug
Runaway History	-0.03	-0.05	-0.07	-0.13	-0.11
Placement History	-0.01	0.06	0.12	0.08	0.32**
Life Events	0.04	-0.09	0.07	0.20	0.11
Total Did Support	-0.02	0.04	0.02	0.04	-0.06
Total Satisfaction	-0.05	0.02	0.03	-0.07	0.02
Network Size	0.04	-0.05	-0.10	-0.09	-0.06
Parent/Guardian	-0.07	0.10	-0.02	-0.02	0.00
Peers in Network	-0.08	-0.10	-0.04	-0.06	-0.06
Number in Network Use Drugs	-0.08	0.09	0.05	0.11	0.11

** $p < .01$

TABLE 14

Intercepts, Betas, and F Ratio for Two Analyses with Each Dependent Measure (Adjustment, Conduct Problems, Substance Abuse, and Sex Risk Taking):

1. Hierarchical Regression Social Support and then Residential Stability.
2. Regression directly on Residential Stability.

	Standardized Beta	F Ratio	DF	Total R
Adjustment				
Social Support		1.3	2, 93	0.03
Enactment (Did)	0.20			
Satisfaction	0.52			
Residential Instability		0.7	4, 91	0.03
Runaway History	0.30			
Placement History	0.42			
Adjustment				
Residential Instability	0.3	2, 144	0.004	
Runaway History	0.56			
Placement History	0.42			
Conduct Problems				
Social Support	0.7	2, 86	0.02	
Enactment (Did)	0.19			
Satisfaction	0.52			
Residential Instability		0.5	4, 84	0.02
Runaway History	0.30			
Placement History	0.41			
Conduct Problems				
Residential Instability	0.4	2, 91	0.01	
Runaway History	0.39			
Placement History	0.28			

TABLE 14 (continued)

	Standardized Beta	F Ratio	DF	Total R
Drug Abuse				
Social Support		0.2	2,86	0.00
Enactment (Did)	0.35			
Satisfaction	0.09			
Residential Instability		2.6*	4,84	0.11
Runaway History	0.07			
Placement History	0.51*			
Residential Instability		5.1**	2, 91	0.10
Runaway History	0.07			
Placement History	0.05			
Sexual Risk Taking				
Social Support		0.4	2, 67	0.01
Enactment (Did)	0.05			
Satisfaction	0.14			
Residential Instability		0.03	4, 65	0.01
Runaway History	0.11			
Placement History	0.84			
Sexual Risk Taking				
Residential Instability		1.8	2, 63	0.03
Runaway History				
Placement History				

*p< .05 **p< .01

stepwise fashion with social support factors entered first followed by the residential instability factors. In order for a significant relationship of residential instability to indirectly impact the dependent measure, both social supports and residential instability would need to account for a significant portion of the variance in the dependent measure.

Only one significant relationship emerged in these regressions. Residential instability has a direct effect on drug use accounting for 11% of the variability of drug use in the sample. However, there is no indirect effect, since social support is not significantly related to substance use and does not add to the significance of the direct relationship of residential instability. No other dependent measure was predicted directly by residential instability or by residential instability indirectly with social support.

Table 15 shows three sets of regressions done with the dependent variables and stressful life events: (a) directly with life events; (b) in a stepwise fashion with residential instability entered first and then stressful life events; and (c) in a stepwise fashion with social supports first and then stressful life events. Life events has no significant direct effect on any of the dependent variables and no indirect effects with either residential stability or social supports. However, when added stepwise to residential instability, its indirect effect on adjustment approaches significance (Standard Beta .10, $p<.07$; $R2 = .06$).

A final set of regressions with social support measures, residential instability, and with life events were done, in which life events scores were viewed as the dependent variable. Table 16 shows regressions done stepwise with social supports entered first and then residential stability, and then life events directly with residential stability. Residential stability showed no significant effect on life events, either directly or with social supports.

In summary, the data prove interesting as a means of better understanding the amount of instability, stress, and adjustment and problem behaviors experienced by runaway and homeless youth. However, social support data are inconsistent, of questionable validity, and raise questions about the usefulness of the variables explored in this study. The hypotheses presented in Chapter 1 regarding the relationships among the four principle variables receive little support.

TABLE 15

Intercepts, Betas and F Ratios for three analyses with each dependent measure(adjustment, conduct problems, drug use, and sex risk taking):

1. Hierarchical regression residential instability then life events
2. Hierarchical regression social support then life events
3. Regression directly on life events

	Standard-ized Beta	F Ratio	DF	Total R
Adjustment				
Residential Instability		0.20	2, 63	0.00
Runaway History	0.49			
Placement History	0.34			
Life Events	0.10*	1.30	3, 62	0.06
Adjustment				
Social Support		0.87	2, 87	0.02
Enactment (Did)	0.22			
Total Satisfaction	0.66			
Life Events	0.10	1.02	3, 86	0.03
Adjustment				
Life Events	1.20	1.60	1, 93	0.02
Conduct Problems				
Residential Instability		0.27	2, 56	0.00
Runaway History	0.55			
Placement History	0.38			
Life Events	0.11	0.37	3, 55	0.02
Conduct Problems				
Social Support		0.88	2, 78	0.02
Enactment (Did)	0.20			
Total Satisfaction	0.64			
Life Events	0.09	0.69	3, 77	0.03

TABLE 15 (continued)

	Standard-ized Beta	F Ratio	DF	Total R
<u>Drug Use</u>				
Residential Instability		4.20	2, 56	0.13
Runaway History	0.08			
Placement History	0.05			
Life Events	0.02	2.90	3, 55	0.14
<u>Drug Use</u>				
Social Support		0.38	2, 78	0.00
Enactment (Did)	0.03			
Total Satisfaction	0.11			
Life Events	0.02	0.28	3, 77	0.01
<u>Drug Use</u>				
Life Events	0.02	0.00	1, 84	0.00
<u>Sex Risk Taking</u>				
Residential Instability		0.06	2, 46	0.00
Runaway History	0.14			
Placement History	0.10			
Life Events	0.03	0.16	3, 45	0.01
<u>Sex Risk Taking</u>				
Social Support		0.17	2, 57	0.01
Enactment (Did)	0.16			
Total Satisfaction	0.04			
Life Events	0.02	0.14	3, 56	0.01
<u>Sex Risk Taking</u>				
Life Events	0.02	0.08	1, 63	0.00

*p< .05

TABLE 16

Intercepts, Betas, and F Ratio for Two Analyses with Life Events Score

1. Hierarchical regression with Social Support and then Residential Instability

2. Regression directly on Residential Instability

	Standard-ized Beta	F Ratio	DF	Total R
Life Events				
Social Support		0.00	2, 59	0.00
Enactment (Did)	0.91			
Satisfaction	0.28			
Residential Instability		1.1	4, 57	0.07
Runaway History				
Placement History				
Life Events				
Residential Instability		1.8	2, 63	0.05
Runaway History	0.67			
Placement History	0.49			

V
Interpretation And Discussion

Chapter 5 returns to the questions about runaway and homeless youth which formed the basis of the design. First, a discussion of the specific research questions and the primary hypotheses presented in Chapter 1 will be presented. In several areas, the data regarding the expected characteristics of the runaway and homeless youth in New York City shelters prove surprising. These findings necessitate interpretation and discussion as they affect assumptions which underlie the study's direction and raise questions about instrumentation. Afterward, the focus will be on more general interpretation of the data gathered in this study about runaway and homeless youth. This interpretation will be centered around three key areas: understanding runaway and homeless youth; recommendations regarding research with runaway and homeless youth; and issues related to program development and service delivery for runaway and homeless youth which emerge from this study.

STRESS IN THIS STUDY

The first basic research question relates to the residential stability measures and whether residential stability is associated with acute stress in the runaway sample. The specific measures which comprise residential stability provide alarming information about runaway youth's histories. More than half of the sample has been placed in an institutional setting at some point in their lives. Almost one in three youth describe themselves as having no home. Youth have averaged three different types of living situations in their lives, with many experiencing numerous different placements and/or multiple experiences in one type of living situation. More than 40% have lived in a group home and 22% in a foster home. About 11% of these runaways describe home as with their parents. Only an additional 29% say home is with either their mother or father.

Only one in five youth is a first time runaway. Approximately one third of the sample has run away more than four times, with the average age of first running away being about 13 years old. The runaway and homeless youth seeking shelter in New York come from predominately single parent families and experience ongoing instability as a part of the experience of growing up. In fact, a substantial majority of youth do not describe their current home with either parent.

Residential instability emerges as two factors, runaway history and placement history, each of which appears a valid, distinct means of evaluating these youth's experience. Runaway history consists of age of first run away episode, number of runaway episodes, and whether or not youth describe themselves as homeless. It focuses specifically on the experience of running away and youth's perception of the impact of this experience. Factor analysis confirmed the face validity of these three measures providing a variable which indicates the seriousness and intensity of runaway history.

Placement history consists of length of time since last at home, number of different types of placements, and institutional experience. It gives a brief indication of the youth's experiences outside of the home, indicating stability of youth's living situations as well as time spent in placement, in the streets, or in informal alternative residential situations. Beyond the measurement of runaway episodes, placement history is an index of what these youth have experienced when out of the home.

In fact, a large subgroup of youth in the shelters was referred from within the child welfare system, the so called "system kids." These youth were in placement or in custody of the public child welfare agency at the time of referral for emergency housing. In terms of the key variables in the study, these "system kids" proved no different than the other youth at the shelters.

The stressful life events scores also indicate that runaway and homeless youth are under great stress in most areas of their lives. The number of recent negative stressors is extremely high when compared with other adolescent populations (Johnson and McCutcheon, 1980; Greenberg, et al., 1983). These adolescents experience acute stress in family, in school, in health, in personal behavior, and among peers.

Increased arguments between youth's parents were experienced in the past 3 months by about half of the sample, and more than 30% say their parents recently separated. Almost one third noted increased parental absence and more than 55% increased conflict with parents. Thirty percent describe changes in parent's financial status and 28% say a parent recently lost his/her job. More than one in six have a parent in legal trouble and almost one in five has a parent who has recently been in jail. Youth indicate that about 40% have a family member with a drug problem and about 30% have an ill or injured family member.

More than 40% of the youth say they have had recent trouble with a teacher and about 40% have had recent trouble with classmates. More than one third have been suspended and 23% expelled. These numbers are not adjusted to eliminate youth who have been out of school for a long period of time. Thus, the percentages of youth experiencing school related stress is likely even higher for the proportion of runaway youth who are currently in school.

When describing recent peer relationships, more than one third indicate ending relationships and more than one third indicate losing a friend. More than one in five has a close friend with a serious drug problem and more than one in four a friend with a serious illness or injury. Many have had trouble with the police (22%) and more than one in four males and one in six females have been jailed. Runaway youth experience high rates of victimization with about 20% having been robbed or burglarized, 13% of the males and 21% of the females having been physically assaulted. More than one in four females and one in seven males say they have been raped or sexually assaulted.

Although residential stability and stressful life events indicate high levels of a type of chronic stress and of acute stress for runaway and homeless youth, there appears to be no association between these two measures of stress. Thus, runaway history and placement history do not provide significant evidence for the theoretical assertion that chronic stress and strain influence the impact of acute stressors. In this population of youth whose lives appear in constant turmoil, residential stability is perhaps too common and too small a part of the chronic stress as experienced by these youth. These youth experience unstable family relationships, school problems, and numerous problems related to poverty, inner cities, and race: numerous stressors which may contribute to chronic stress. Residential stability appears not to have a significant impact on acute stress in a context of so many stressors.

In fact, it appears that the runaway and homeless youth in this sample may have more in common with youth living in similarly stressful conditions in New York than to the runaways found in many other studies, a proposition that will be further discussed later in this chapter. This would reinforce the view that residential instability as a type of chronic stress may not be an important factor in determining response to acute stress or in affecting other psychosocial characteristics of runaway and homeless youth.

SOCIAL SUPPORT NETWORKS

A second basic question relates to the characteristics of social support networks of runaway and homeless youth. As this domain has not been targeted in previous studies of runaway and homeless youth, this study provides new and unique information about social supports. The findings of this study related to the size of networks (social embeddedness), the types of interactions (social enactment), and need for and satisfaction with support (perceived support) raise questions about the utility of current instruments in assessing the social support networks of these youth.

Runaway youth show great variability in the size, nature and utilization of their support networks. Although there are youth in the sample with few supports, most of these runaways describe a surprising number of supports available in the past month. Runaways name an average two persons to whom they have gone for intimate support, three persons to whom they have gone for physical or material support, and four persons to whom they have gone for socializing support. Male runaways include more than nine individuals in their networks and females include more than seven. Runaways' social networks do not appear significantly smaller than those of youth in other studies (Barrera, 1981; McGowan and Kohn, 1990).

In attempting to understand the findings related to social networks, it is essential to raise concerns about runaway youth's understanding and interpretation of supportive relationships. Lack of permanence in relationships and coping in hostile environments appear to result in the inclusion of acquaintances and even strangers in the network. In piloting the social support instrument, so many youth included staff and youth from the shelter in which they had been staying less than 48 hours that the questions had to be revised to focus on supports before entering the shelter. Nearly one quarter of the sample described the shelter as home, a fact which may further indicate a unique, troubling perspective on social connections. The runaway youth's experiences may result in a unique cognition of social interactions and, thus, decrease the value of the measure of social network size as a means of understanding their social supports.

Less than one in four youth included their father and slightly more than half included their mother as part of their social support network. Approximately two out of three included a parent or other adult relative in their support network. Thus, while these youth indicate available supports, they appear to rely largely on peers, with many youth's networks devoid of parents or parent figures.

Comparable data regarding parents' inclusion in support networks is difficult to find due to the many distinct measures used to evaluate social supports. In a large sample of early adolescents, Blyth et al. (1982) found that more than 9 out of 10 adolescents listed one or both parents as significant in their lives. McGowan and Kohn (1990), in their study of pregnant teenagers in New York City using a version of the ASSIS, found that more than 70% included their mothers and more than 50% included their fathers in their social support network. Clearly many adolescents do not use parents as a primary source of support, although the runaway population appears even less reliant on parents than most adolescents.

The data on perceived support also present an unclear picture of these adolescents' social supports and raise questions about the usefulness of this variable with the runaway and homeless population. Youth show moderate need for social supports and high satisfaction with the supports which they receive. Given their histories, it might be expected that youth would be less satisfied with their supports or that there would be evidence that satisfaction with supports would relate to total network size or data on who is available in their social network. In fact, satisfaction did not relate to network size, and only satisfaction with intimate supports related to the number of persons who provided intimate support. There are also no significant relationships between satisfaction and the number of peers in the network or whether or not a parent or parent figure is included in the network.

The satisfaction scores obtained in this sample of runaway and homeless youth, while surprisingly high, appear consistent with data obtained by other researchers with similar populations (McGowan and

Kohn, 1990; Rotheram-Borus, Rosario and Koopman, 1991). Perhaps youth who have been homeless, many of whom have been frequently displaced and thrown out of families and institutions, have little means of evaluating the adequacy of supports or their satisfaction with them. Perhaps these youth have lowered expectations and "requirements" which reflect the development of increased alienation and hopelessness. In any case, data from this sample confirm that adolescents' perception of supports as reflected in need and satisfaction may be of limited utility among runaways.

There were limited indications of gender differences in social supports. Females had smaller support networks than males but a similar percentage of their networks were made up of peers and of parent or parent figures. The fact that males' networks show greater drug and alcohol use reflects gender differences among most adolescent samples (Kandel and Davies, 1982). There is no indication that the relationships between social support network variables selected for this study differ by gender. In fact, there is little evidence of significant relationships among any of the network variables for the entire sample. The social support data by itself appears to reveal little about the impact of these youth's experiences.

ADJUSTMENT AND BEHAVIOR PROBLEMS

Base rates among this runaway and homeless youth sample for adjustment and problem behaviors provide unexpected results compared with recent studies of the mental health of apparently similar populations (Mundy et al., 1990; Yates et al., 1988). The youth in New York City shelters shows less depression and have higher self-esteem than was expected while displaying behavior problems and risky behaviors at the high rate anticipated. After discussing the base rates for individual variables, the balance of this section will explore possible interpretations of these findings.

Mean depression scores (M = .99, SD = .88) on the SCL-90 do not appear significantly higher than those Derogatis (1983) found in general adolescent sample (M = .80, SD = .88). As expected, female scores on depression are higher than male scores, although both groups have scores which do not appear substantially higher than the general sample of adolescents. Individual items indicate that specific youth experience current and at times acute distress. More than 13% of the youth have thoughts of ending their lives quite a bit or extremely often. Feelings of hopelessness were experienced by more than one in three youth in the week of the interview and more than 12% felt hopeless quite a bit or extremely often. These findings are consistent with base rates for severe depression of 5-15% and of 20-40% found among minority youth (Gibbs, 1990).

The Rosenberg Self Esteem scores reveal a population with moderately high self-esteem (30.2 on a scale of 40) and a moderate standard deviation of 5.6. Although often used, it is difficult to find comparable scoring on the Rosenberg Self-Esteem. However, when the mean scores are compared to those found in other studies (Rosenberg, 1965; Rosenberg and Pearlin, 1978; Barnes and Farrier, 1985), using the percentage of highest possible score as a mark, runaway and homeless youth whose mean is about 75% of the highest possible score, appear to have relatively high self-esteem. They do not show low self-esteem as a result of instability and homelessness. Self-esteem and depression are highly correlated as youth who are depressed also have low self-esteem.

Although conduct problems were assessed, the study did not attempt to diagnose conduct disorder in individual youth. However, there are clear indications that this population has high rates of conduct problems. First, we can estimate prevalence of youth who would meet diagnostic criteria by reviewing how many youth appear to have the required number of behavioral indicators for a conduct disorder diagnosis. Estimates were done with the understanding that the runaway item (more than two episodes) was removed from our measure of conduct problems. Based on the behaviors reported, nearly one in three youth in the study would receive a conduct disorder diagnosis according to DSMIIIR criteria (DSMIIIR). An analysis of the first 150 runaway and homeless youth in the larger study on HIV risk, from which this sample was taken, revealed that 32% meet DSMIIIR criteria for a conduct disorder diagnosis (Rotheram-Borus and Rosario, 1990).

The individual items on the Conduct Problem Scale also provide powerful evidence of a population with specific behavioral problems. In the past 3 months, more than 70% of the runaways have been in a physical fight and almost 40% of these youth have been in three or more fights. One in four has bullied younger children and one in seven has destroyed someone else's property. More than 60% have been truant and more than 40% have been in trouble in school more than three times.

Regular drug use (more than three times a month) is described by more than one in five youth and regular alcohol use by nearly one in three. In fact, 23% of the males and 13% of the females say they have a current drug or alcohol problem. A recent study which analyzed data about drug and alcohol use among these youth found 27% using either alcohol or drugs at least once a week during the past 3 months (Koopman, Rosario, and Rotheram-Borus, 1993). This same study found that the runaways use alcohol substantially more than drugs and that marijuana (43%), cocaine/crack (19%), and hallucinogens (14%) were the drugs most often used.

Rates of drug use among the runaway youth is alarming. In comparison to a national household sample of adolescents (National Institute of Drug Abuse, 1991) these youth are three times more likely to have ever used marijuana (43% vs. 15%), seven times more likely to use cocaine/crack (19% vs. 2.6%), and five times more likely to use hallucinogens (14% vs. 3.3%). Clearly substance abuse is a major problem for runaway and homeless youth, a fact made particularly disturbing by building evidence that it increases risk for HIV infection (Koopman, Rosario, and Rotheram-Borus, 1994).

The data show sex risk behavior to be high among runaway and homeless youth. A recent analysis of sex risk behaviors (Koopman, Rosario, and Rotheram-Borus, 1993) provides details about the sexual behaviors of this population of runaway and homeless youth. More than 60% of runaways are currently sexually active with opposite sex partners, with a median of 1.0 partners ($M = 1.9$; $SD = 2.3$) for females and 3.0 partners ($M = 4.5$; $SD = 6.2$) for males. There is great variability of number of partners with a substantial minority of these youth having sex with multiple partners during recent months. Only about half of these encounters are protected by condom use ($M = .47$; $SD = .42$ for penile-vaginal intercourse).

Jessor's theory of problem behaviors (1977) receives limited support from the data. Conduct disorder shows a strong relationship to both drug use and sex risk taking. However, in these data there is no significant relationship between sex risk taking and drug use as might be anticipated. Depression and self-esteem measures relate highly to each other but not to conduct disorder or drug use. Only sex risk taking behavior correlates significantly with conduct disorder, depression, and self-esteem. However, while correlating with higher levels of depression and conduct disorder as anticipated, it also correlates with higher self-esteem. Perhaps a degree of self-esteem is necessary as a prerequisite for meeting and responding to potential sex partners.

Nevertheless, the significant relationships between sex risk taking and other measures of adjustment and behavior problems may reflect that risky sex can result from several personal sources. For youth on the street it can be a means of escape from distressful feelings or feelings of loneliness. For others it may be a matter of survival, of securing food and shelter. Feelings of hopelessness and lack of future have been consistently found to relate to early sexual intercourse and teen pregnancy (Hofferth, 1987; Dryfoos, 1990).

The high rates of sexual victimization among these youth may result in patterns of sexual behavior which reflect the psychological results of incest, sexual abuse, and rape. Clinical wisdom and anecdotal information provide evidence of the relationship between sexual victimization and the use of sexual contacts as a means of finding desired emotional support and establishing self worth. Clearly these data indicate the depth of the challenge for those interested in decreasing sex risk taking among runaway and homeless youth.

In reviewing the findings related to adjustment and behavior problems, it is striking that the adjustment measures of depression and self-esteem revealed relatively normal rates while the behavior problems appeared at the high rates expected. There are several possible explanations for these findings which contrast with those of recent studies of runaway youth.

First, most recent studies of runaway and homeless youth were done in other cities, such as Los Angeles (Mundy et al., 1990; Robertson et al., 1988; Yates et al., 1988) and often with youth who were on the street or in clinics rather than in shelters. It may be that a different population is seen receiving services in shelters or even that 48 hours of shelter and safety changes the responses of youth who may feel more stable and more hopeful. However, a key factor in the differences in the findings appears to be geographic location and the ethnicity, race, and social experience of the youth seeking services in different locations. In the Los Angeles based studies, white youth comprise the largest ethnic group in each of the studies by a substantial margin. Many youth in these studies are originally from outside Los Angeles, from smaller cities and towns in the west and Midwest. This study of youth in New York City runaway shelters is basically a sample of minority youth, with two out of three participants African-American, about one-quarter hispanic, and 7% bi-racial. Since less than 4% was either white or Asian, this is basically a study of African-American and hispanic youth from New York City, most of whom come from the inner city.

In reviewing the literature related to the mental health of African-American youth, it becomes evident that the runaways in this study appear to have more in common with these youth than samples from other runaway studies. In the area of self-esteem, research has been clear in dismissing racial differences. Recent studies indicate that the self-esteem and self-concepts of African-American youth are as positive or more positive than samples of white youth (Gibbs, 1985; Powell, 1985; Rosenberg and Simmons, 1971; Taylor, 1976).

Studies of depression among youth have revealed little difference in rates of depression (Goldberg, 1981; Kandel and Davies, 1982; Gibbs, 1985; Kaplan, Hong and Weinhold, 1984; Schoenbach et al., 1983) between African-Americans and whites. Control for socio-economic status was emphasized in some but not all of these studies. In a general population study comparing whites and minority groups, Frerichs et al. (1981) found that membership in a minority group had little influence on the prevalence of depressive symptoms. Vernon and Roberts (1982) found higher rates of lifetime major depression among whites and Mexican-Americans than African-Americans and current rates of major depression to be similar.

Although the rates of depression appear similar for minority youth, many question the validity of measures of depression based on observed differences in symptom expression. Studies have reported that depressed African-American patients express more anger and hostility and less feeling of hopelessness (Raskin and Crook, 1975). African-American adolescents have been found more likely to discuss somatic complaints instead of complaining about dysphoric mood (Axelson, 1985; Abepieme, 1982). In fact, the external focus of African-American youth's symptoms of depression may be related to the rates of depression found in the sample as well as to the high rates of behavior problems.

Externalizing anxiety and depression has been linked to hyperactivity and aggression among younger African-American children and a pattern of delinquency, substance abuse, and sexual promiscuity in older youth (Gibbs, 1990; Gibbs, 1982; Franklin, 1982). Feelings of depression can be expressed as anger, hostility, and rage (Aguilera and Messick, 1978). Felton and Jamison (1986) suggest that African-American youth present affect related illness "characterized by greater degrees of anger, hostility, denial, and self-destructive behavior (such as drug use and antisocial acts)." Myers (1989) points out that African-American youth, particularly males, are over-represented in diagnoses of disorders of adjustment, conduct, and socialization, a fact which may come from an externally focused depressive syndrome among African-American adolescents.

African-American youth have higher rates of delinquency related behaviors (Children's Defense Fund, 1985); have high rates of school drop-outs, particularly among inner city youth (U.S. Census Bureau, 1987); high rates of teen pregnancy (Children's Defense Fund, 1988; Chilman, 1983); and are more likely than white teenagers to be diagnosed with conduct disorder (Dembo, 1988). The externalizing of depression and anxiety which result in hostile, angry, self-destructive behaviors may be one explanation for these rates.

High rates of conduct problems and risk behaviors may also be explained by theories related to social environment and deviance that emphasize the experience of minority youth in the world of the inner city. In describing delinquent behavior, Weiner (1982) differentiates delinquency related to psychopathology from socio-cultural delinquency. A significant amount of African-American delinquency is viewed as socio-cultural, that is a product of culturally defined or situationally determined processes and norms of behavior. Many theories view antisocial behavior as related to disadvantaged class or ethnic position (Braithewhite, 1981; Rutter and Giller, 1983) or as a reaction to individual's experiences in the neighborhood social environment. Peoples and Loebor (1994) found that once individual factors were accounted for, ethnicity showed no relationship to delinquency although residence in an underclass neighborhood was significantly related. Thus, antisocial behavior is a response to lack of educational or occupational opportunity (Cloward and Ohlin, 1960) or an indication of strain created by discrepancies between achievement aspirations and expectations (Dembo et al., 1986; Dembo et al., 1979; Oetting and Beauvais, 1987).

Behaviors are viewed as influenced by survival in a neighborhood and school (Hannerz, 1969; Liebow, 1967) and by peer and neighborhood characteristics that may include drug use (Dembo et al, 1994; Dembo et al., 1986), negative attitudes toward school (Harrington, 1989) and racial mistrust (Biafora et al, 1993). Meyers (1989) and Rosella et al (1993) suggest an urban stress model in which the relationship between minority adolescents and the various qualities of the social environment is reciprocal and complex. The environment provides a context in which children experience poverty and negative social experiences. The environment creates tremendous stress which increases risk for a variety of mental health disorders. The rates of behavior problems found in the runaway sample in this study may reflect the social experience of these youth in the inner city more than the runaway experience. Perhaps the high rates of behavior problems result from the general experience and concomitant stress of these youth as well as from the additional stress of residential instability. The ethnic, racial, and cultural context appears to confound any findings related to the stress of running away in this population, and also to distinguish it from most other runaway samples.

THE THEORETICAL MODEL

The analytic procedures conducted to assess the relationships among the four domains of the study--residential instability, stressful life events, social supports, and adjustment and problem behaviors--do not support the theoretical model which is presented in Figure 1. Regression analyses revealed only one relationship which is statistically significant. Placement history correlates with drug use. This finding, rather than providing support for the model presented on stress and problem behavior, may support theories about the importance of the social environment. Perhaps being away from home, changing living situations, and especially institutional placements result in greater exposure to drugs and greater vulnerability to drug use.

Hierarchical regressions performed among domains do not show evidence of the relationships among residential stability, stressful life events, and adjustment and behavior problems. There is no evidence of the buffering effect of social supports on either residential instability or stressful life events and adjustment and behavior problems. Nor is there evidence that residential stability and stressful life events work together to influence adjustment and behavior problems.

Several considerations appear important in reviewing the lack of evidence of the importance of social supports and stress measures in this sample. First is the relative homogeneity of the population. Runaway youth have high rates of residential instability, acute stress, and adjustment and behavior problems. It was anticipated that these youth would present rates that would be clustered and thus significant results would be difficult to obtain. Greater variance of youth in the sample, including runaways and nonrunaways, might show more meaningful results in determining relationships between stress, life events, and behavior.

The lack of significant relationships between social supports and adjustment and behavior problems may be explained in several ways. Each explanation assumes that runaways' perceptions and expectations of social supports may be impaired or misleading. The most simplistic is that the degree of psychopathology found in runaway youth is associated with limited ability to trust, form meaningful relationships, and ultimately to evaluate accurately social attachments. Shaffer and Caton (1984) have emphasized that runaways have extremely high rates of psychopathology. Psychiatric disorders of childhood and adolescence have been found to relate to many patterns in these youth's lives, including problems with parents, numerous changes of placements, and high rates of risk behaviors (Rotheram-Borus, Koopman and Ehrhardt, 1991). Perhaps behavior problems and psychopathology influence their understanding of and reliance on social supports while also contributing to the instability of their living situations.

Attachment theory which emphasizes early parental attachments as influencing child development and psychological health, as well as later relationships and social functioning (Bowlby, 1969) might explain the ability of youth to assess the nature of their relationships and their perception of the value of social supports. Studies of the quality of attachment as a factor in emotional and behavior responses to the social environment have supported the important influence of early attachment on latency age children's social behavior (Weiss, 1991), on family and parenting behavior, and on adult relationships (Grossmann and Grossmann, 1991). Recently, Penzero and Lein (1995), in applying attachment theory to the behavior ofadolescents in foster care, found patterns of alienation caused by frequent drifting between homes and frequent transitions to be the experience of many youth diagnosed with conduct disorder. As runaway youth have histories which include continuous instability, evidence of inconsistent parenting, histories of parental substance problems, and high rates of physical and sexual abuse, it is possible that social supports are less important due to alienation and lack of ability to form strong attachments. This would result in runaways having limited perception of need and limited ability to gauge the strength and utility of social relationships.

Finally, a more salient means of explaining the limited importance social supports and, indeed, most acute stressors may be Maslow's hierarchy of needs (Maslow, 1968). He described physiological needs relating to hunger, rest, and warmth as primary and safety needs such as stability, security, protection, and freedom from fear as second in determining motivation. Belonging and loving needs which focus on relationships with peers and partners, as well as esteem needs and self-actualization, become important only as the need for physical comfort and safety are met. Clearly, for most runaway and homeless youth there is an ongoing focus on getting physical needs met through the street culture, changing residences, or seeking emergency shelter. In addition, safety needs, for which parents and parental figures provide a principal source, remain unmet as youth live unstable, often fearful lives. Social support relationships, even if perceived correctly by runaways, may be of limited importance due to the more basic needs which continually remain unmet. Thus, only after more basic needs have been met would social supports have the potency to mediate the effects of stress.

Ultimately the lack of significant findings regarding the importance of stress and social supports likely reflects the chronicity and complexity of runaway and homeless youth's problems as well as the intricate interplay of social and physical environment, ethnicity and social class, personality, and behavior. From an ecological perspective such as discussed by Bronfenbenner (1979) and emphasized in certain social work literature (Germaine and Gitterman, 1980), the effort to isolate variables related to relationships and experience is risky and potentially of limited value. The evidence that the runaways in this study are more like their neighborhood peers than runaways from other places, with different life experiences, reinforces this assertion. Better definitions of variables and more distinct and comprehensive measures of social supports, stress, and behavior might result in significant results but still be of little help in the development of strategies to change the lives of runaway and homeless youth.

RUNAWAYS AND HIGH-RISK ADOLESCENT BEHAVIORS

Given these negative results on the primary hypotheses of this study, the balance of this discussion will focus on understanding what this exploratory study reveals about the experiences of runaway youth and about directions for future research and programming. One means of providing a context for understanding the serious effects of the life experiences of runaways is to focus on what is known about the antecedents of several high risk adolescent behaviors: delinquency; substance abuse; and behaviors related to related to sexual activity, i.e. early sexual intercourse, failure to use contraception, and early childbearing.

Dryfoos (1991) has reviewed antecedents of these risk behaviors, and there is compelling evidence that the life experience of runaway and homeless youth make them more likely than most youth to display each of these adolescent behaviors.

Basic demographic characteristics of the runaways in this study relate to these troubling behaviors. As noted previously, delinquency, early initiation of sexual intercourse, and early childbearing have been related to poverty; and delinquency and substance abuse have been linked to living in urban neighborhoods of high density. The runaway and homeless youth in this study are overwhelmingly from poor families and from high density neighborhoods in New York City. Personal characteristics which have been found to relate to delinquency include low expectations and low achievement in school as well as truancy (Dryfoos, 1991). Large numbers of runaway and homeless youth describe school problems and truancy. Acting out behaviors such as fighting and lying and general aggressivity relate to delinquent behavior and these appear at high rates in the assessment of conduct problems. Youth who are much influenced by peers are at greater risk for delinquency (Hawkins and Fraser, 1984; Burke and Weir, 1978; Vondra and Garbarino, 1988). Runaways have few consistent parent supports and rely heavily on peers for all types of social supports.

Family antecedents of delinquency include lack of bonding, abusive behavior, and poor communication (Dryfoos, 1991; Burgess, Anderson and Schellenbach, 1988; Jessor and Jessor, 1977). In this context, runaways' histories of physical and sexual abuse, their continuous instability, as well as the lack of parental support evident in their social support networks is alarming. High risk behaviors in families such as criminality, violence, and alcoholism--behaviors which are often reported in runaways' families--also have been linked to eventual involvement in delinquent behaviors (Dryfoos, 1991).

Many of these experiences and characteristics are also antecedents of substance abuse. Poor school performance and truancy (Hawkins and Lishner, 1987); conduct problems (Donovan and Jessor;) heavy peer influence (Huba et al., 1980; Gorusch and Butler, 1976; Kandel, Kessler, and Margulies, 1978) and lack of parental support (Jessor and Jessor, 1977; Hawkins and Fraser, 1984) have been related to subsequent substance abuse. Parental substance abuse and early initiation to drug and alcohol use have been demonstrated as antecedents of substance abuse. Two out of five runaways have a family member with a current drug problem, and evidence of extremely early initiation into substance use is emerging (Koopman, Rosario, and Rotheram-Borus, 1992). In addition, both stress and depression have been linked to substance abuse in adolescents. Certainly runaways who have enormous amounts of both chronic and acute stress and whose rates of depression are above those of most adolescents would be expected to develop high rates of substance abuse.

Antecedents of early sexual intercourse, failure to use contraception, and early childbearing include little hope for future prospects, low school grades, and lack of parental support and communication (Hooferth, 1987). Each of these behaviors is influenced heavily by peer norms and attitudes. Early sexual intercourse has been related to delinquent behaviors, substance abuse, and truancy; and both early sexual intercourse and early childbearing is more common in youth from single headed households. Runaway youth demonstrate many of the antecedents of sexual risk taking behavior and describe family and support systems which correlate highly with the development of these behaviors.

The data on residential stability, stressful life events, and social supports clearly indicate that runaway and homeless youth are a population whose lives include numerous antecedents of risk behavior in addition to running away. Indeed, each domain of this study reveals information which places these youth at great risk in various ways. Although the data did not show direct relationships between these domains, the study of stress and social support networks still provides unique, powerful evidence that these youth can be expected to have multiple problems based on both past and current experiences. Furthermore, it makes clear the need for intervention models which recognize the breadth of runaways' problems and the implications of lengthy histories of negative and potentially devastating experiences.

RECOMMENDATIONS FOR SERVICE DELIVERY

The following recommendations emerge from the results of this study:

Early Intervention

Runaways seeking shelter services have already established patterns of instability and of behaviors which make successful intervention difficult. The most general risk factors which these youth experience relate to poverty, slums, and lack of hope - issues which currently overwhelm minority young people in our largest cities. However, there are indications that these youth are in trouble at an early age; and individual, family, and social problems escalate during adolescence, resulting in running away and in an array of risk behaviors.

Although many youth and their families become involved with the child welfare system or community service providers, it is critical that better prevention and intervention be done while children are still with parents. Youth's histories of child abuse, of moving from place to place, and of family problems related to drugs and alcohol show that runaway behavior is the culmination of failure on the part of the schools, health providers, and child welfare providers to intervene adequately with these youth.

The mean age at runaways' first episode is about 13 years old. Although described as an adolescent risk behavior, running away clearly has its roots in pre-adolescent experience and emerges as a child's response to experiences of early adolescence. The fact that runaway behavior relates so highly to other problem behaviors of adolescence demonstrates the need for holistic approaches to children. Preventive services, including family support, advocacy, drug prevention, educational support, and skills building for these children and their families are necessary. Even for youth who are developing signs of psychopathology, early intervention can provide parents, teachers, and especially children themselves with needed coping strategies and relevant treatment.

Improvements In Foster Care

The challenges of providing adequate child welfare services to growing numbers of children and youth have long been documented. The fact that so many runaways and homeless youth have been in foster care placements and are known to the "system" reflects the struggles of the child welfare system with issues of permanency, of providing care to the more troubled children and adolescents, the lack of foster families able to manage teenagers, and the lack of effective residential treatment strategies for many children and youth.

Three specific areas of concern emerge from this study of runaway and homeless youth. First, the fact that so many of the youth at runaway shelters are "system kids" (27%) who have been placed in shelters due to lack of emergency beds within the child welfare system reflects the current inability of the child welfare system to adequately respond to the needs of a large number of youth in crisis. Although residence in a runaway shelter while a placement is sought may currently be the safest, most therapeutic response to a youth's housing needs, clearly this drains the limited resources for youth who are not currently under the guardianship of the child welfare system. It underscores the need for a better emergency response within the "system" and the need to more quickly find and facilitate appropriate placements for "system" youth.

Clearly the plight of "system kids" also reflects the lack of adequate long-term placements and intervention strategies for adolescents who demonstrate multiple adjustment and behavior problems including patterns of running away. As children in the foster care system become older, they become more difficult to place. As some of these youth move from place to place, personality and behavior problems become exacerbated. The failure of the child welfare system to make inroads in tackling the need for both family and institutional placements that can work successfully with these difficult youth is demonstrated by the fact that the number of "system kids" in New York City shelters continued to grow through the 1980s. This has resulted in several programs limiting the availability of housing for youth who have open cases in the New York State Child Welfare Agency.

A last specific problem in the child welfare system that has become evident through the experiences of runaway shelters is the need for youth who are leaving placements to be adequately prepared for independent living. Many youth in the study have been through foster care placements and been discharged without necessary skills to live on their own or to cope with largely unsupportive home environments. Youth need basic skills such as budgeting, cooking, how to look for work, and what to expect from employers, as well as general skills related to problem solving, assertiveness, and interpersonal relationships.

Runaway Services

Two primary areas for program development in runaway services emerge from this study. The first relates to the breadth of services offered when youth seek services at shelters and the second relates to the need for longer-term approaches to meet the needs of runaway and homeless youth. It should be noted that runaway shelters have always been defined as providing a full range of services, but limited funding has always limited the ability of most programs to provide the quality and quantity of services required by their clients.

Comprehensive Intervention Strategies

Runaways have many different problems, starting with the need for food, shelter, and safety, and including problems with health, mental health, families, education, and the legal system. Available services must include intervention with substance abuse, sexual risk taking, and patterns of behavior which result in continuous homelessness. Given histories of instability and the suspicion that social connections are often tenuous, it is critical that the crisis model of runaway shelters include efforts to engage youth quickly in holistic interventions aimed at meeting multiple needs and addressing multiple problems.

Crisis theory and crisis intervention strategies emphasize that crises result in a loss of equilibrium and potential openness to change (Parad and Parad, 1990; Rappaport, 1965). Runaways and homeless youth who seek shelter may be running away from home for the first or second time because of a precipitant related to parents, peers, or school which has upset a previously existing balance. Homeless youth seeking shelter from the street may have become frightened by an incident of violence or ill from a medical problem or lack of an adequate diet. Clearly many youth arrive at shelters at a point when a skilled offer of help might succeed in starting to break long standing patterns of instability and poor coping. Runaway shelters must be equipped to provide the services necessary in an effective way.

Networking with other service providers is one means of beginning to meet this challenge. Linkages with providers of mental health services, drug treatment, health care, family treatment, and educational assessment and services exist in many shelters but needs to be built into the both the model and the funding of runaway programs. Demonstration projects have demonstrated the utility of establishing formal linkages between runaway shelters and mental health and health providers (Rotheram and Bradley, 1991). Surveys of shelters' needs and recommendations of national organizations such as the National Association of Social Workers (1992) and National Network of Runaway and Youth Services (1991) indicate the need for a greater range of available services.

A second means of providing more comprehensive interventions is to strengthen the capacities of shelters to provide broader services. Demonstration projects for improving intervention with drug use, family problems, and suicide risk have been supported by specific federal and state grants. Yet the challenge of maintaining these services and making them available in all runaway sites has not been met.

Many of the needs of runaway youth while in shelters go unmet due to the lack of programming and the lack of skilled personnel to provide intervention. Shelters have received little fiscal support for staff training and for development of professional staff positions. However, recognition of the need for comprehensive services and the need to staff services with appropriately trained staff has been growing. A National Association of Social Workers monogragh on runaway youth (1992) states "Providers obviously have decided they need professionals, because there are no federal requirements for professionally trained staff" (p. 66) and concludes that in developing an array of services at shelters "It may be useful to group these services into basic components (for example, outreach, health, education, and counseling) and to identify the staffing needs (professional and nonprofessional) of each component" (p. 66).

Long-Term Services

The chronic stress and continuous instability of runaway and homeless youth, as well as the adjustment and behavior problems which they develop, necessitate services which go beyond those of the runaway shelter. Recognition that many youth have no homes or placements to which to return and that these youth lack the independent living and coping skills to be successful in the community has resulted in the development of transitional living programs. Although relatively new on a nation-wide basis, these longer-term residences have become a critical part of runaway service delivery.

Aftercare services have been offered by runaway shelters since their inception. However, limited resources have resulted in limited services offered for limited periods of time to youth whose lives generally remain stressful and chaotic. Given the complexity and longevity of runaways' problems, even more substantial aftercare does not seem a sufficient response. Perhaps a system of case management or community support for youth who are not currently being served in the child welfare system would prove effective in increasing stability and support for youth.

Case management as a model providing continuity and supports has proven somewhat effective in enabling persons who are chronically mentally ill to maintain stability in the community (Fariello and Scheidt, 1988; Rife et al., 1991; Rubin, 1992). Runaway youth who return home, to independent living, or even the streets might benefit from the support and advocacy of a case manager who maintains active participation in providing services over time. These youth's multiple problems, both situational and behavioral, require ongoing counseling, skills building, referrals and advocacy. The lack of stability in runaway and homeless youth's lives might be decreased by the consistency of a skilled worker providing individualized support.

Although the importance of social supports in decreasing poor adjustment and behavior problems is not shown by the data of this study, the relationship between peer behaviors such as drug use and individual youth's drug use is apparent. Part of the challenge of services to these youth at high risk is to help them develop more positive peer supports, ones that will reinforce positive behaviors. Strategies which help youth to create support for positive behaviors, particularly from peers, could be a program priority for shelter and transitional living. For example, peer support groups which last beyond the provision of shelter services could be developed to support practicing safer sex and remaining chem free. Self-help models including 12-step programs could provide models from which to develop longer-term peer based interventions.

IMPLICATIONS FOR FUTURE RESEARCH

The limitations of the sample used in this study have been discussed in Chapter 3. This is a specific runaway sample from specific shelter sites in New York. Future research about runaways must continue to be specific about samples because clearly there are many different populations of runaway and homeless youth.

The lack of significant findings related to the relationships among stress, social supports, and adjustment and behavior does little to clarify the already contradictory evidence related to stress and the modifying influence of social supports. If such a modifying influence exists, research with a more heterogeneous sample might better demonstrate its effects. The usefulness of chronic stress as a variable requires further investigation and, perhaps, better definition.

In order to understand the relationship of personality, social supports, and stress, a longitudinal design would be necessary. Relationships that emerge from the cross-sectional design have no predictive value. Thus, is one can not determine the degree to which runaways' behavioral difficulties have an impact on their residential histories or the degree to which instability results in increased maladjustment. The surprisingly large social networks and the high satisfaction with social supports of unstable and troubled youth raise questions about the usefulness and validity of the assessment of social supports with runaway and homeless youth.

A research design could be developed aimed at tracking instability, stress, and youth's descriptions of social supports over time, a design with a control group from similar backgrounds in order to better identify the specific impact of residential instability. However, based on the limited findings of this preliminary study, the cost of such a study, and the vast needs of runaways this type of study does not seem worthwhile.

Future research might focus in two distinct directions: toward a more full understanding of the experience of runaway youth and on developing and evaluating effective intervention strategies. To more fully understand the experience of this population of youth will require longitudinal studies akin to those of Fanshel (Fanshel et al., 1989; Fanshel et al., 1991) with youth in the foster care system and will require more successful efforts to define complex variables and to conduct multivariate studies. Perhaps, given the complexity and changeability of these youth's lives and the difficulty of getting and maintaining useful samples, more qualitative research designs would provide increased understanding. Certainly, ethnographic studies might better explain the runaway experience and help service providers and program designers to develop more successful interventions in neighborhoods, at street hangouts, and with peer groups.

The development and evaluation of effective interventions aimed at decreasing risk behaviors and increasing coping skills is a second important direction for research. Studies evaluating interventions with suicide and depression (Rotheram-Borus and Bradley, 1991) and sexual risk taking (Rotheram-Borus and Koopman, 1991; Rotheram-Borus, Koopman, and Ehrhardt, 1991) have been undertaken. Research which focuses on effective strategies aimed at increasing youth's residential stability is certainly needed.

Clearly, this study indicates the seriousness of runaway and homeless youth's plight and the wisdom of putting resources into attempts to provide a range of services to these adolescents. As an attempt to pull apart these youth's complex and tangled experience, this study has been partially successful. The effort to find significant factors in determining the impact of runaway behavior on youth's coping and adjustment proved unsuccessful. However, information about social supports, adjustment and behavior problems as well as about these youth's histories were explored and described in unique detail.

Bibliography

Adams, G., Gullotta, T., & Clancy, M. (1985). Homeless Adolescents: A Descriptive Difference Between Runaways and Throwaways. *Adolescence*, 20, 714-724.

Allen, D., Lehman, S., Green, T., and Lindgren, M.L., (1994) *HIV Among Homeless Adults and Runaway Youth, United States*, 1989-1992. AIDS 8(11) 1593-1598

American Medical Association Council on Scientific Affairs, (1989). Healthcare Needs of Homeless and Runaway Youths. *Journal of the American Medical Association*, 262, 1358-1361.

Adebiempe, V. (1981). Overview: White Norms and Psychiatric Diagnosis of Black Patients. *American Journal of Psychiatry*, 138, 279-285.

Aneshensel, C.S. & Frerichs, R. (1982). Stress, Support, and Depression: A Longitudinal Causal Model. *Journal of Community Psychology*, 10, 307-315.

Aquilera, D. & Messick, J. (1978*). Crisis Intervention: Theory and Methodology. St. Louis*: C.V. Mosby.

Axelson, J. (1985). *Counseling and Development in a Multicultural Society*. Monterey, CA: Brooks/Cole.

Bachman, J. & Johnston, L.(1978*). The Monitoring the Future Project: Design and Procedures.* Ann Arbor, MI: Ann Arbor Institute for Social Research, University of Michigan.

Barden, J, (1990, February 5). Strife in Families Swells Tide of Homeless Youths. *New York Times.*

Barnes, M., And Farrier, S. A (1985). Longitudinal Study of the Self Concept of Low-Income Youth. *Adolescence*, 20, 199-205.

Barrera, M. (1981). Preliminary Development of a Scale of Social Support. *American Journal of Community Psychology*, 9, 435-447.

Barrera, M. (1981). *Social Support in the Adjustment of Pregnant Adolescents: Assessment Issues.* In Gottlieb, B. H. (Ed.), Social Networks and Social Support. Beverly Hills, CA: Sage.

Barrera, M. (1986). Distinctions Between Social Support Concepts, Measures, and Models. *American Journal of Community Psychology,* 14(4), 413-445.

Barrera, M. & Ainlay, S. (1983). The Structure of Social Support: A Conceptual and Empirical Analysis. *Journal of Community Psychology,* 11,133-143.

Berkman, I. & Syme, S. (1979). Social Networks, Host Resistance and Mortality: A Nine Year Follow-Up Study of Alameda County Residents. *American Journal of Epidemiology,* 109, 186-204.

Biafora, F., Frank, A., Warheit, G., Zimmerman, R., and Gil, A. (1993) Racial Mistrust and Deviant Behaviors Among Ethnically Diverse Black Adolescent Boys. *Journal of Applied Social Psychology* 23(11) 891-910

Blascovich, J. & Tomaka, J. (1991). Measures of Self Esteem. In Robinson, J, Shaver,P., & Wrightsman, L. (Eds.), *Measures of Personality and Social Psychological Attitudes: Volume 1.* San Diego: Academic Press.

Bowlby, J. (1969). *Attachment and Loss: Volume 1.* New York: Basic Books.

Braithewaite, J. (1981) The Myth of Social Class and Criminality Reconsidered. *American Sociological Review,* 43, 36-57.

Brand, A. & Johnson, J. (1982). *Note on the Reliability of the Life Events Checklist. Psychological Reports,* 50, 1274.

Braucht, G.N., Brakarsh, D., Follingstad, D. & Berry, K. (1973) Deviant Drug Use In Adolescence: A Review of Psychosocial Correlates. *Psychological Bulletin,* 79, 92-106.

Brennan, T. (1980). Mapping the Diversity among Runaways. *Journal of Family Issues,* 1, 189-207.

Brennan, T., Huizinga, D., & Elliot, D.S. (1979) *The Social Psychology of Runaways.* Lexington, MA: Lexington Books.

Brim, J. (1974). Social Network Correlates of Avowed Happiness. *Journal of Nervous and Mental Disease,* 58, 432-439.

Broadhead,W. , Kaplan, B., Et Al. (1983) The Epidemiological Evidence for a Relationship between Social Support and Health. *American Journal of Epidemiology,* 117, 521-537.

Bronfenbrenner, U., (1979). *The Ecology of Human Development: Experiments by Nature and Design.* Cambridge, MA: Harvard University.

Bucy, J. (1987) Prepared Statement of June Bucy, Executive Director, The National Network of Runaway and Youth Services. In the *Crisis In Homelessness: Effects on Children and Families. Washington: Hearing Before the Select Committee on Children, Youth and Families, U.S. House of Representatives.*

Bucy, J. & Obolensky, N. (1990). Runaway and Homeless Youth. In Rotheram- Borus, M.J., Bradley, J., & Obolensky, N. (Eds.), *Planning to Live: Evaluating and Treating Suicidal Teens In Community Settings.* Tulsa: National Resource Center for Youth Services.

Burgess, R., Anderson, E. & Schellenbach, C. (1988). A Social Interactional Approach to the Study of Abusive Families. In Vincent, J. (Ed.), *Advances in Family Interaction, Assessment, and Theory: Vol. 2.* Greenwich, CT: JAI Press.

Burke R. J. & Weir, T. (1978). Sex Differences in Adolescent Life Stress, Social Support, and Well Being. *Journal of Psychology*, 98, 277-288.

Caplan,G. (1974). *Support Systems and Community Mental Health: Lectures on Concept Development.* New York: Behavioral Publications.

Cassel, J. (1976). The Contribution of the Social Environment to Host Resistance. *American Journal of Epidemiology*, 104, 107-123.

Cassel, J. Psychosocial Processes and Health. *International Journal of Public Health*, 4, 471-482

Cauce, A., Felner, R., & Primavera, J. (1982). Social Support in High Risk Adolescents: Structural Components and Adaptive Impact. *American Journal of Community Psychology*, 10, (4), 417-428.

Chelimsky, E. (1982, May 5). The Problem of Runaway and Homeless Youth. In *Oversight Hearing on Runway and Homeless Youth Program.* Washington: Subcommittee on Human Resources, Committee on Education and Labor, U.S. House of Representatives.

Cherry, A. (1993) *Combining Cluster and Discriminant Analysis to Develop a Social Bond Typology of Runaway Youth Research on Social Work Practice* 3(2) 175-190

Chicago Coalition for the Homeless Position Paper, (1985*)*. *Youth Homelessness in Chicago. Chicago:* Youth Subcommittee of the Chicago Coalition for the Homeless.

Children's Defense Fund, (1985*)*. *Black and White Children In America.* Washington, DC.

Children's Defense Fund, (1988). *A Children's Budget FY 1989: An Analysis of Our Nation's Investment In Children.* Washington, DC.

Children's Defense Fund, (1988). *Teens and AIDS: Opportunities for Prevention.* Washington, DC.

Chilman, C. (1983). *Adolescent Sexuality In a Changing American Society.* New York: John Wiley.

Citizen's Committee for Children of New York, (1983). *Homeless Youth In New York City: Nowhere to Turn.* New York: Citizens Committee for Children of New York and the Runaway and Homeless Youth Advocacy Project.

Cloward, R. and Ohlin, L., (1960). *Delinquency and Opportunity: A Theory of Delinquent Gangs.* Glencoe, IL: Free Press.

Cobb, S. (1976). Social Support as a Moderator of Life Stress. *Psychosomatic Medicine*, 38, 300-314.

Cohen S. & Hoberman, H.M. (1983) Positive Events and Social Supports as Buffers of Life Change Stress. *Journal of Applied Social Psychology*, 13, 99-125.

Collins, A. & Pancoast, D. (1976*)*. *Natural Helping Networks. Washington*, DC: National Association of Social Work.

Colten, E. & Gore, S. (1991*)*. *Adolescent Stress: Causes and Consequences.* New York: Aldine De Gruyer.

Compass, B. (1987). Coping with Stress During Childhood and Adolescence. *Psychological Bulletin*, 101, 1-11.

Compass, B. & Wagner, B. (1991). Psychosocial Stress During Adolescence: Intrapersonal and Interpersonal Processes. In Colten, M. & Gore, S. *Adolescent Stress: Causes and Consequences.* New York: Aldine De Gruyter.

Compass, B., Slavin, L., Wagner, B. & Vannatta, K. (1986). Relationship of Life Events, and Social Support with Psychological Dysfunction among Adolescents. *Journal of Youth and Adolescence*, 15(3), 205-221.

Condry, J. & Siman, M. (1974). Characteristics of Peer- and Adult-Oriented Children. *Journal of Marriage and Family*, 56, 543-554.

Crespi, T ., and Sabatelli, R. (1993) Adolescent Runaways and Family Strife: A Conflict-Induced Differentiation Framework. *Adolescence* 28(112) 867-878

Damon, W. (1983). *Social and Personality Development*. New York: W.W. Norton.

D'angelo, R. (1984). Effects Coincident with the Presence or Absence of a One-Shot Interview Directed at Families of Runaways. *Journal of Social Service Research,* 8, 71-81.

Dean, A. & Lin, N. (1977). The Stress Buffering Role of Social Support: Problems and Prospects for Systematic Investigation. *Journal of Nervous and Mental Disease,* 165, 403-417.

De Man, A., Dolan, D. Pelletier, R. and Reid, C. Adolescent Runaways: Familial and Personal Correlates. *Social Behavior and Personality* 21(2) 163-167

Deman, A., Dolan, D., Pelletier, R., and Reid, C. (1994) Adolescent Running Away Behavior: Active or Passive Avoidance*? Journal of Genetic Psychology*, 155(1) 59-64

Dembo, R. (1988). Delinquency among Black Male Youth. In Gibbs, J. (Ed.), *Young, Black and Male in America: An Endangered Species.* Dover, MA: Auburn House.

Dembo, R., Blount, W., Schmeidler, J, & Burgos, W. (1986). Perceived Environmental Drug Use Risk and Correlates of Drug Use and Non-Use among Inner City Youths: The Motivated Actor. *International Journal of the Addictions,* 21, 977-1000.

Deman, A., Dolan, D., Pelletier, R., and Reid, C. (1994) Adolescent Running Away Behavior: Active or Passive Avoidance? *Journal of Genetic Psychology*, 155(1) 59-64

Dembo, R., Farrow, D., Schmeidler, J. & Burgos, W. (1979). Testing a Causation Model of Environmental Influences on Early Drug Involvement of Inner City Junior High School Youths. *American Journal of Alcohol Abuse,* 6, 313-336.

Demo, D. (1985). The Measurement of Self Esteem: Refining Our Methods. *Journal Of Personality and Social Psychology*, 48, 1490-1502.

Derogatis, L. (1977).   SCL-90 Administration, Scoring, and
    Procedures Manual.   Towson, MD: *Clinical Psychometric*
    Research.

Derogatis, L. & Cleary, P. (1977). Confirmation of the Dimensional
    Structure of the SCL-90: A Study in Construct Validation.
    Journal of Clinical Psychology, 33, 981-989.

Derogatis, L., Lipman, R., & Covi, L. (1976).   An Outpatient
    Psychiatric Rating Scale: A Preliminary Report. In Guy, W.
    (Ed.), *ECDEU Assessment Manual.*

Derogatis, R., Lipman, R., Covi, L. & Rickels, K. (1972). Factorial
    Invariance of Symptom Dimensions in Anxious and Depressive
    Neuroses. *Archives of General Psychiatry*, 155.

Derogatis, L., Lipman, R., Rickels, K., Ulenruth, E., and Covi, L.
    (1973). The Hopkins Symptom Checklist (HSCL): A Measure
    of Primary Symptom Dimensions.   In Pichot, P. (Ed.),
    Psychological   Measurement: Modern   Problems   In
    Pharmacopsychiatry. Basel: S.Karger.

Dignam, T, Barrera, M. , & West, S. (1986). Occupational Stress,
    Social Support, and Burnout among Correctional Officers.
    American Journal of Community Psychology, 14, 117-193.

Dobson, G., Goudy, K., and Powers, E. (1979). Further Analysis of
    Rosenberg's Self-Esteem Scale. *Psychological Reports*, 44, 639-
    641.

Dohrenwrend, B.P. & Dohrenwrend, B.S. (1969*).   Social Status and*
    Psychological Disorder. New York: Wiley.

Dohrenwrend, B.S. (1973).   Life Events as Stressors: A
    Methodological Inquiry.   *Journal of Health and Science*
    Behavior, 14, 167-75.

Dohrenwrend, B.S., (1973). Social Status and Stressful Life Events.
    Journal of Personality and Social Psychology, 28, 225-35.

Dohrenwrend, B.S., Dodson, M., Dohrenwrend, B.P. & Shrout, P.
    (1984). Symptoms, Hassles, Social Supports, and Life Events:
    Problem of Confounded Measures. *Journal of Abnormal*
    Psychology, 93, 222-230.

Donovan, J. & Jessor, R. (1985). Structure of Problem Behavior in
    Adolescence and Young Adulthood. *Journal of Consulting and*
    Clinical Psychology, 53(6), 890-904.

Dryfoos, J., (1990). *Adolescents at Risk: Prevalence and Prevention.*
    New York: Oxford University Press.

Englander, S.W. (1984). Some Self-Reported Correlates of Runaway Behavior in Adolescent Females. *Journal of Consulting and Clinical Psychology*, 52, 484-485.

English, C. (1973). *Leaving Home: A Typology of Runaways.* Society., 10, 22-24.

Fanshel, D. & Shinn, B. (1978). *Children in Foster Care.* New York: Columbia University.

Fanshel, D., Finch, S., & Grundy, J. (1989). Modes of Exit from Foster Care and Adjustment at Time of Departure of Children with Unstable Life Histories. *Child Welfare*, 68(4), 391-403.

Fanshel, D., Finch, S., & Grundy, J. (1990). *Foster Children in Life Course Perspective*, New York: Columbia University.

Farber, E., Hinast, C., Mccoard, D., & Folkner, M. (1984). Violence in Families of Adolescent Runaways. *Child Abuse and Neglect*, 8, 295-299.

Fariello, J. & Scheidt, S. (1988). Clinical Case Management of the Dually Diagnosed Patient. *Hospital and Community Psychiatry*, 40, 1065-1067.

Felton, E. & Jamison, A. (1986). Suicidal Behavior in American Blacks. In Klerman, G. (Ed.), *Suicide and Depression among Adolescents and Young Adults.* Washington, DC: American Psychiatric Press.

Ferran, E. & Sabitini, A. (1985). Homeless Youth: the New York Experience. *International Journal of Family Psychiatry*, 6, 117-128.

Fisher, D. , Wilson, P., Queen, M. (1995) Sexual and Drug Taking Experiences Reported By Runaway Youth. *Journal of Alcohol and Drug Education* 40(2) 88-99

Fleming, J. & Courtney, B. (1984). The Dimensionality of Self-Esteem. A Hierarchical Facet Model for Revised Measurement Scales. *Journal of Personality and Social Psychology*, 46, 404-421.

Franklin, A. (1982). Therapeutic Interventions with Urban Black Adolescents. In Jones, E. & Korchin, S. (Eds.), *Minority Mental Health.* New York: Praeger.

Friedman, A. & Clickman, N. (1987). Effects of Psychiatric Symptomatology on Treatment Outcome for Adolescent Male Drug Users. *Journal of Nervous and Mental Disease*, 175, 425.

Gad, M.J. & Johnson, J.H. (1980). Correlates of Adolescent Stress as Related to Race, S.E.S. and Perceived Levels of Social Support. *Journal of Clinical Child Psychology*, 9(1) 13-16.

Germaine, C. & Gitterman, A. (1980*). A Life Model of Social Work Practice*. New York: Columbia University Press.

Gersten, J., Langner, T., Eisenberg, J. & Simcha-Fagan, O. (1977). An Evaluation of the Etiologic Role of Stressful Life-Change Events in Psychological Disorders. *Journal of Health and Social Behavior*, 18, 228-244.

Gibbs, J. (1986). Assessment of Depression in Urban Adolescent Females: Implications for Early Intervention Strategies. *American Journal of Social Psychiatry*, 6, 50-56.

Gibbs, J. (1990). Mental Health Issues of Black Adolescents. In Stiffman, A. & Davis, L. (Eds*.), Ethnic Issues in Adolescent Mental Health*. Newbury Park, CA: Sage Publications.

Gibbs, J. (1982). Personality Patterns of Delinquent Females: Ethnic and Sociocultural Variations. *Journal of Clinical Psychology*, 38, 198-206.

Gibbs, J. (1985). Psychosocial Factors Associated with Depression in Urban Adolescent Females: Implications for Assessment. *Journal of Youth and Adolescence*, 14, 47-60.

Golan, N. (1978), *Treatment in Crisis Situations*. New York: Free Press.

Goldberg, E. (1981*). Depression and Suicide Ideation in the Young Adult*. American Journal of Psychiatry, 138, 35-40.

Goldstein, Y., Freud, A., & Solnit, A. (1973*). Beyond the Best Interests of the Child*. New York: Free Press.

Gonzalez, J. (1994) *A Model of Social Work Services for Runaway and at Risk Youth in Texas*. Doctoral Dissertation at University of Texas

Gordan, J. (1975). The Washington D.C. Runaway House. *Journal of Community Psychiatry*, 3, 68-80.

Gore, S. (1978). The Effects of Social Support in Moderating the Health Consequences of Unemployment. *Journal of Health and Social Behavior*, 19, 157-165.

Gorsuch,R. & Butler, M. (1976). Initial Drug Use: A Review of Predisposing Social Psychological Factors. *Psychological Bulletin*, 83,120-137.

Greater Boston Emergency Network (1985). *Ride a Painted Pony on a Spinning Wheel.* Boston: Massachusetts Committee for Children and Youth.

Greenberg, M., Siegal, J., & Leitch, C. (1983). The Nature and Importance of Attachment Relationships to Parents and Peers During Adolescence. *Journal of Youth and Adolescence*, 12, 373-386.

Grossman, K. & Grossman, K. (1991). Attachment Quality as an Organizer of Emotional and Behavioral Responses in a Longitudinal Perspective. In Parks, C., Stevenson-Hinde, J., & Marris, P. (Eds.), *Attachment across the Life Cycle.* New York: Tavistock/Rutledge.

Gullota, T. (1979). *Leaving Home: Family Relationships of the Runaway Child.* Social Casework, 60, 111-114.

Hannerz, V. (1969). *Soulside.* New York: Columbia University.

Harrington, W. (1989, August 27). *Hopes and Dreams.* Washington Post Sunday Magazine, 17-39.

Hawkins, J. & Fraser, M. (1984). Social Network Analysis and Drug Misuse. *Social Service Review*, 58, 81-97.

Hawkins, J. & Lishner, D. (1987). Etiology and Prevention of Antisocial Behavior in Children and Adolescents. In Crowell, D., Evans, I., & O'Donnells, C. (Eds.), *Childhood Aggression and Violence.* New York: Plenum.

Hawkins, J., Jenson, J., Catalano, R., & Lishner, D. (1988). Delinquency and Drug Use: Implications for Social Services. *Social Service Review*, 62, 258-284.

Hensley, W. (1977). Differences between Males and Females on Rosenberg Scale of Self Esteem. *Psychological Reports*, 41, 829-830.

Hermann, R. (1988). Center Provides Approach to Major Social Ill: Homeless Urban Runaways, "Throwaways." *Journal of the American Medical Association*, 260, 311-312.

Hersch, P. (1988, January). Coming of Age in the Streets. *Psychology Today*, 28-37.

Hinkle, L.E. (1974). The Effect of Exposure to Cultural Change, Social Change, and Changes in Interpersonal Relationships on Health. In Dohrenwrend, B. & Dohrenwrend, B. (Eds.), *Stressful Life Events: Their Nature and Effects.* New York: Wiley.

Hirsch, B. (1980). Natural Support Systems and Coping with Major Life Changes. *American Journal of Community Psychology*, 8, 159-172.

Hofferth, S. (1987). Factors in Initiation of Sexual Intercourse. In Hofferth, S. & Hayes, C., *Risking the Future: Adolescent Sexuality, Pregnancy, and Childbearing*. Washington, DC: National Academy Press.

Hofferth, S. & Hayes, C. (1987). *Risking the Future: Adolescent Sexuality, Pregnancy, and Childbearing* (Vols. 1 & 2). Washington, DC: National Academy Press.

Holmes, T. & Rahe, R. (1967). The Social Readjustment Rating Scale. *Journal of Psychosomatic Research*, 11, 213-218.

Homer, L.E. (1973). Community-Based Resource for Runaway Girls. *Social Casework*, 54, 473-479.

Hotaling, G.T., Atwell, S.G., & Linsky, A. (1978). Adolescent Life Changes and Illness: A Comparison of Three Models. *Journal of Youth and Adolescence*, 7, 393-403.

Huba, G., Wingard, J. & Bentler, P. (1980). Longitudinal Analysis of the Role of Peer Support, Adult Models, and Peer Subculture in Beginning Adolescent Substance Abuse: An Application of Set-Wise Canonical Correlation Methods. *Multivariate Behavioral Research*, 15, 259-279.

Hudgens, R.W. (1974). Personal Catastrophe and Depression: a Consideration of the Subject with Respect to Medically Ill Adolescents, and a Requiem for Retrospective Life Event Studies. In Dohrenwend, B. & Dohrenwend, B. (Eds.), *Stressful Life Events: Their Nature and Effect*. New York: Wiley.

Hudson, R., Petty, B., Freeman, A., Haley, C., & Krepcho, M. (1989). Adolescent Runaway's Behavioral Risk Factors, Knowledge About AIDS and Attitudes About Condom Usage. *Abstracts of the V International Conference on AIDS*, (P. 728). Ottawa, Ontario, Canada: International Research Development Center.

Hulsey, T. & White, R. (1989). Family Characteristics and Measures of Behavior in Foster and Non-Foster Children. *American Journal of Orthopsychiatry*, 59(4), 502-509.

Institute of Medicine. (1988). *Homelessness, Health, and Human Needs*. Washington, DC: National Academy Press.

Jaegers, R. and Mock, L. (1993) Culture and Social Outcomes among Inner-City African American Children: An Afrographic Exploration. Special Issue: Emotional Development of African-American Children. *Journal of Black Psychology* 19(4) 391-405

Janus, M. Archembualt, F., Brown, S. and Welsh, L. (1995) Physical Abuse in Canadian Runaway Adolescents. *Child Abuse and Neglect* 19 (4)

Janus, M., Mccormack, A., Burgess, A., & Harmon, C. (1987). *Adolescent Runaways: Causes and Consequences.* Lexington, MA: Lexington Books.

Jessor, R. & Jessor,S. (1977). *Problem Behavior and Psychosocial Development: A Longitudinal Study of Youth.* New York: Academic Press.

Johnson, J.H. & Mccutcheon, S. (1980). Assessing Life Events in Older Children and Adolescents: Preliminary Findings with the Life Events Checklist. In Sarason, I. & Spielberger, C. (Eds.*)*, *Stress and Anxiety: Vol. 7.* Washington, DC: Hemisphere.

Jones, L. A (1988). Typology of Adolescent Runaways. *Child and Adolescent Social Work,* 5, 16-29.

Jorgensen, S., King, S., & Torrey, B. (1980, February). Dyadic and Social Network Influences on Adolescent Exposure to Pregnancy Risk. *Journal of Family and Marriage*, 141-155.

Kandel, D. & Davies, M. (1982). Epidemiology of Depressive Mood in Adolescents. Archives of General Psychiatry, 39, 1205-1212.

Kandel, D., Kessler, R., & Margulies, R. (1978). Antecedents of Adolescent Initiation Into Stages of Drug Use. In Kandel, D. (Ed.), *Longitudinal Research on Drug Use: Empirical Findings and Methodological Issues.* Washington, DC: Hemisphere.

Kandel, D., Simcha-Fagan, O., & Davies, M. (1986). Risk Factors for Delinquency and Illicit Drug Use From Adolescence to Adulthood. *Journal of Drug Issues*, 16, 67-70.

Kaplan, S., Hong, G.K., Weinhold, C. (1984). Epidemiology of Depressive Symptomatology in Adolescents. *Journal of the Academy of Child Psychiatry*, 23, 91-98.

Kashani, J., Goodard, P., & Ried, J. (1989). Correlates of Suicidal Ideation In a Community Sample of Children and Adolescents. *Journal of the American Academy of Child and Adolescent Psychiatry*, 28, 912-917.

Kashubeck, S., Pottebaum, S., and Read, N. (1994) Predicting Elopement From Residential Treatment Centers. *American Journal of Orthopsychiatry* 64(1) 126-135

Kelly, P. & Kelly, V. (1985). Supporting Natural Helpers: A Cross-Cultural Study. *Social Casework*, 358-367.

Koopman, C., Rosario, M., and Rotheram-Borus, M. (1994) Alcohol and Drug Use and Sexual Behaviors Placing Runaways at Risk for HIV Infection. *Addictive Behaviors* 19(1) 95-103

Koopman, C., Rosario, M. & Rotheram-Borus, M. (In Press). Alcohol and Drug Use and Sexual Behaviors Placing Runaways at Risk for HIV Infection. *Journal of Adolescence.*

Kufelt, K. & Nimo, M. (1987). Youth on the Street: Abuse and Neglect in the Eighties. *Child Abuse and Neglect*, 11, 531-543.

Kurtz, P., Jarvis, S. & Kurtz, G. (1991). Problems of Homeless Youth: Empirical Findings and Human Service Issues. *Social Work*. 36, 309-314.

Kurtz, P., Kurtz, G. & Jarvis, S. (1991). Problems of Maltreated Runaway Youth. *Adolescence*, 26, 543-555.

Lazarus, R. (1966). *Psychological Stress and the Coping Process.* New York: Mcgraw Hill.

Leslie, S. (1974). Psychiatric Disorders in the Young Adolescents of an Industrial Town. *British Journal of Psychiatry*, 125, 113-124.

Levine, R., Metzendorf, D., and Van Boskirk, K. (1986). Runaway and Throwaway Youth: A Case for Early Intervention with Truants. *Social Work in Education*, 8, 93-106.

Libertoff, K. (1980). The Runaway Child in American History: A Social History. *Journal of Family Issues*, 1, 151-164.

Liebow, E. (1967*). Tally's Corner: A Study of Negro Street Corner Men*. Boston: Little Brown.

Lin, N., Simeone, R., Ensel, W.M., & Kuo, W. (1979). Social Support, Stressful Life Events and Illness: A Model and an Empirical Test. *Journal of Health and Social Behavior*, 20, 108-119.

Lorr, M. & Wunderlich, R. (1986). Two Measures of Self-Esteem. *Journal of Personality Assessment*, 50, 18-23.

Maslow, A. (1968). *Towards a Psychology of Being (2nd Ed.).* Princeton, NJ: Van Nostrand Press.

Mathews, L. & Ilon, L. (1980). Becoming a Chronic Runaway. *Family Relations*, 29, 404-409.

Mccormack, A., Janus, M-D., & Burgess, A. (1986). Runaway Youths and Sexual Victimization. *Child Abuse and Neglect*, 10, 387-395.

Mcgowan, B. & Kohn, A. (1990). Social Support and Teen Pregnancy in the Inner City. In Stiffman, A.R. & Davis, L. (Eds.), *Ethnic Issues in Adolescent Mental Health*. Newbury Park, CA: Sage Publications.

Mechanic, D. (1974). Social Structure and Personal Adaptation: Some Neglected Dimensions. In Coehlo, G., Hamburg, D. & Adams, J. (Eds.) *Coping and Adaptation*. New York: Basic Books.

Mechanic, D. (1975). Problems in the Measurement of Stress and Social Readjustment. *Journal of Human Stress*, 1, 43-48.

Meyer-Bahlburg, H., Ehrhardt, A., Exner, T., & Gruen, R. (1988). *Sexual Risk Behavior Assessment Schedule-Youth*. New York: New York State Psychiatric Institute and Department of Psychiatry, College of Physicians and Surgeons of Columbia University.

Miller, D. & Lin, E. (1988). Children in Sheltered Homeless Families: Reported Health Status and Use of Health Services. *Pediatrics*, 81, 668-673.

Miller, D., Miller, D., Hoffman, F., & Duggan, R. (1980). Runaways: Illegal Aliens in Their Own Land. Brooklyn, N.Y: Praeger Publishers.

Mitchell, R. & Hodson, C. (1983). Coping with Domestic Violence: Social Support and Psychological Health among Battered Women. *American Journal of Community Psychology*, 11,629-654.

Morgan, O. (1982). Runaways, Jurisdiction, Dynamics and Treatment. *Journal of Marital and Family Therapy*, 8, 121-127.

Moses, A., (1978). The Runaway Youth Act. *Social Service Review*, 52, 227- 243.

Mullis,R., Youngs,G., Mullis, A., Rathge, R. (1993) Adolescent Stress: Issues of Measurement. *Adolescence*, 28(110), 267-279

Mundy, P., Robertson, M., Robertson, J., & Greenblatt, M. (1990). The Prevalence of Psychotic Symptoms in Homeless Adolescents. *Journal of the American Academy of Child and Adolescent Psychiatry*, 29, 724-731.

Myers, H. (1989). Urban Stress and Mental Health in Black Youth: An Epidemiologic and Conceptual Update.   In Jones, R. (Ed.), *Black Adolescents*. Berkeley, CA: Cobb and Henry.

National Association of Social Workers. Helping Vulnerable Youths: *Runaway and Homeless Adolescents in the United States*, Author, Washington D.D., 1992

National Network of Runaway and Youth Services (1991). *to Whom Do They Belong? Runaway, Homeless, and Other Youth in Risk Situations in the* 1990s. Washington D. C.

New York City Youth Board (1988). *Report on Runaway and Homeless Youth in New York City*. Unpublished.

Newcomb, M., Huba, G., & Bentler, P. (1981). A Multidimensional Assessment of Stressful Life Events among Adolescents. *Journal of Health and Social Behavior*, 22, 400-415.

Nye, I. (1980). Theoretical Perspective on Running Away. *Journal of Family Issues*, 1, 274-279 .

Oetting, E. and Beauvais, F. (1987). Common Elements in Drug Use: Peer Clusters and Other Psychological Factors. *Journal of Drug Issues*, 17, 133-151.

Olsen, L. (1982, Spring). Predicting the Permanency Status of Children in Foster Care. *Social Work Research and Abstracts*, 9-20.

Parad, H. & Parad, L. (1990). Crisis Intervention: An Introductory Overview. In Parad, H. & Parad, L. (Eds.), *Crisis Intervention Book 2: The Practitioners Book for Brief Therapy*. New York: Family Service Association.

Parcel, G., Nader, P. & Meyer, M. (1977). Adolescent Health Concerns: Problems and Patterns of Utilization in Tri-Ethnic Urban Populations. *Pediatrics,* 60, 157-164.

Pardeck, J. (1982). *The Forgotten Children: A Study of the Stability and Continuity of Foster Care*. Washington, D.C. : University Press of America.

Pardeck, J. (1985). Profile of the Child Likely to Experience Unstable Foster Care. *Adolescence,* 20(79), 690-696.

Paton, S. & Kandel, D. (1978). Psychological Factors and Adolescent Illicit Drug Use: Ethnicity and Sex Differences. *Adolescence,* 13, 187-200.

Pattison, E. (1977). A Theoretical-Empirical Base for Social System Therapy. in Feulks, E., Wintrob, J., Westmeyer, J. & Favazza,

A. (Eds.), *Current Perspectives in Cultural Psychiatry.* New York: Spectrum.

Pearlin, L., Menaghan, E., Lieberman, M., & Mullen, J. (1981) The Stress Process. *Journal of Health and Social Behavior*, 337-356.

Pennbridge, J., Freese, T & Mackenzie, R. (1992). High-Risk Behaviors among Male Street Youth in Hollywood, California. *AIDS Education and Prevention*, (Fall Suppl.), 24-33.

Penzerro, R. and Lein, L (1995). Burning Their Bridges: Disordered Attachment and Foster Care Discharge. *Child Welfare* 74 (2), 351-366

Peoples, F. and Loeber, R. (1994) Do Individual Factors and Neighborhood Context Explain Ethnic Differences in Juvenile Delinquency? *Journal of Quantitative Criminology* 10 (2) 141-157

Pietropinto, A. (1985). Runaway Children. *Medical Aspects of Human Sexuality*, 19, 175-189.

Post, P. and Mccoard, D. (1994) Needs and Self Concept of Runaway Adolescents. *School Counselor* 41(3) 212-219

Powell, G. (1985). Self-Concepts among Afro-American Students in Racially Isolated Minority Schools: Some Regional Differences. *Journal of the American Academy of Child Psychiatry*, 24, 142-149.

Powers, J., Eckenrode, J., & Jacklitch, B. (1990). Maltreatment among Runaways and Homeless Youth. *Child Abuse and Neglect*, 14, 87-98.

Price, V. (1987). Runaway and Homeless Street Youth. In the Boston Foundation (Ed.), *Homelessness: Critical Issues for Policy and Practice.* Boston: the Boston Foundation, 24-28.

Proch, K. & Taber, M. (1987, Summer). Alienated Adolescents in Foster Care. *Social Work Research and Abstracts*, 9-13.

Rahe, R. (1974). The Pathway Between Subject's Recent Life Changes and Their Near-Future Illness: Reports, Representative Results and Methodological Issues. In Dohrenwrend, B.S. & Dohrenwrend, B.P. (Eds.), *Stressful Life Events: Their Nature and Effects.* New York: Wiley.

Rapaport, L. (1965). The State of Crisis: Some Theoretical Considerations. In Parad, H. (Ed.), *Crisis Intervention: Selected*

Readings. New York: Family Service Association.

Rapoport, R. (1965). Normal Crises, Family Structure, and Mental Health. In Parad, H. (Ed.), *Crisis Intervention: Selected Readings.* New York: Family Service Association.

Raskin, A. & Crook, T. (1975), Psychiatric History and Symptom Differences in Black and White Depressed Inpatients. *Journal of Consulting,* 43, 73-80.

Reynolds, W. (1988). Measurement of Academic Self-Concept in College Students. *Journal of Personality Assessment,* 52, 223-240.

Rife, J., First, R., Greenlee, R., Miller, I. & Feichter, M. (1991). Case Management with Homeless Mentally Ill People. *Health and Social Work,* 16, 58-67.

Robertson, J., Koegel, P., & Ferguson, L. (1988). *Alcohol Use and Abuse among Homeless Adolescents In Hollywood.* Paper Presented at the American Public Health Association, Boston, MA.

Robertson, M. (1989). *Homeless Youth: An Overview of the Literature.* Paper Presented at the National Conference on Homeless Children and Youth, Washington, DC.

Rodriguez, O & Zayas, L. (1990). Hispanic Adolescents and Antisocial Behavior: Sociocultural Factors and Implications. In Stiffman, A. & Davis L. (Eds.), Ethnic Issues in Adolescent Mental Health. Newbury Park, CA: Sage Publications.

Rohner, R. & Rohner, E. (1980). Antecedents and Consequences of Parental Rejection: A Theory of Emotional Abuse. *Child Abuse and Neglect,* 4, 189-198.

Rosenberg, M.(1965). *Society and the Adolescent Self Image. Princeton,* NJ: Princeton University Press.

Rosenberg, M. & Pearlin, L. (1978). Social Class and Self Esteem among Children and Adults. *American Journal of Sociology,* 84(1), 53-77.

Rosenberg, M., Schooler, C., & Schoenbach, C. (1989). Self-Esteem and Adolescent Problems: Modeling Reciprocal Effects. *American Sociological Review,* 54, 1004-1008.

Rosenberg, M. & Simmons, R. (1971). Black and White Self-Esteem: *The Urban Child.* Washington, DC: Rose Monograph Series.

Rosella and Albrecht, S. (1993) Toward an Understanding of the Health Status of Black Adolescents: An Application of Stress-

Coping Framework. *Issues In Comprehensive Pediatric Nursing* 16(4) 193-205

Rotheram-Borus, M. (1989). Evaluation of Suicide among Youth in Community Settings. *Suicide and Life Threatening Behaviors,* 19, 361-374.

Rotheram-Borus, M. (1989). *Reducing Sexual Behaviors Which Place Runaway and Gay Youth at Risk for AIDS: A Preliminary Report.* Paper Presented at Child Psychiatry Grand Rounds, New York State Psychiatric Institute, New York, NY.

Rotheram-Borus, M. (1990). *HIV Prevention among Adolescents.* Presentation at Conference on Pediatric AIDS, Washington, DC.

Rotheram-Borus, M. and Bradley, J. Triage Model for Suicidal Runaways. *American Journal of Orthopsychiatry,* 1991, 6, 122-127

Rotheram-Borus, M. & Koopman, C. (1989). The Triple a Project: Adolescent AIDS Awareness for Runaway and Gay Youth, a Preliminary Report. *Multicultural Inquiry and Research on AIDS,* 3(1), 4-5.

Rotheram-Borus, M., Koopman, C., & Bradley, J. (1989). Barriers to AIDS Prevention Programs with Runaway Youth. In Woodruff, J., Doherty, D., & Athey, J. (Eds.), *Troubled Adolescents and HIV Infection: Issues in Prevention and Treatment.* Washington, DC: National Institute of Mental Health.

Rotheram-Borus, M., Rosario, M., & Koopman, C. (1991). Minority Youth at High Risk: Gay Males and Runaways. In Colten, M. & Gore, S. (Eds.), *Adolescent Stress: Causes and Consequences.* New York: Aldine De Gruyer.

Rothman, J. (1989). Intervention Research: Application to Runaway and Homeless Youth. *Social Work Research and Abstracts,* 13-18.

Rothman, J. & David, T. (1985*). Status Offenders in Los Angeles County: Focus on Runaway and Homeless Youth (a Study and Policy Recommendations).* Los Angeles, CA: School of Social Welfare, University of California, Los Angeles.

Rubin, A. (1992). Is Case Management Effective for People with Serious Mental Illness? *Health and Social Work,* 17, 138-150.

Rubin, C., Rubenstein, J., Stechler, G., Heeren, T., Halton, A., Housman, D., and Kasten, L. (1992) Depressive Affect in

"Normal" Adolescents: Relationship to Life Stress. *American Journal of Orthopsychiatry* 62(3), 430-441

Runyon, D. & Gould, C. (1985). Foster Care for Child Maltreatment: Impact on Delinquent Behavior. *Pediatrics,* 75(3), 562-568.

Rutter, M. & Giller, H. (1983*). Juvenile Delinquency: Trends and Prospects.* Baltimore, MD: Penguin.

Samsa, D., Masten, A., & Ramirez, M. (1990*). Adjustment of Adolescents in Homeless Families.* Poster Presented at the Society for Research on Adolescents Conference, Atlanta, GA.

Sandberg, D., Rotheram, M., Bradley, J. & Martin, J. (1988). Methodological Issues in Assessing AIDS Prevention Programs with Adolescents. *Journal of Adolescent Research*, 3, 413-418.

Sandler, I. (1980). Social Support Resources, Stress, and Maladjustment of Poor Children. *American Journal of Community Psychology*, 8, 41-52.

Sarason, I., Monchaux, C., & Hunt, T. (1975). Methodological Issues in the Assessment of Life Stress. In Lev, L.(Ed*.), Emotions: Their Parameters and Measurement.* New York: Rover.

Sarason, I., Johnson, J., & Siegel, J.(1978). Assessing the Impact of Life Changes: Development of the Life Experience Survey. *Journal of Consulting and Clinical Psychology*, 46, 932-946.

Schilling, R. (1987, March). Limitations of Social Support. *Social Service Review*, Vol 61 No. 1.

Schoenbach, V., Kaplan, B., Grimson, R., & Miller, F. (1983). Prevalence of Self-Reported Depressive Symptoms in Young Adolescents. *American Journal of Public Health*, 73, 1281-1287.

Selye, H. (1976). *Stress in Health and Disease.* Boston: Butterworth.

Shaffer, D. & Caton, C. (1983). *Runaways and Homeless Youth in New York City.* Report to the Ittleson Foundation, New York, NY.

Shaffer, D., Garland, A., Gould, M., Fisher, P. & Trautman, P. (1988). Preventing Teenage Suicide: A Critical Review. *Journal of the American Academy of Child and Adolescent Psychiatry*, 114, 675-687.

Shalwitz, J., Goulart, M., Dunnigan, K., & Flannery, D. (1990). Prevalence of Sexually Transmitted Diseases and HIV in a Homeless Youth Medical Clinic in San Francisco. *Presentation at the Sixth Annual International Conference on AIDS*, San Francisco, CA.

Shane, P. (1989). Changing Patterns among Homeless and Runaway Youth. *American Journal of Orthopsychiatry*, 59, 206-214.

Shireman, J. (1983). Achieving Permanence After Placement. In Mcgowan, B. & Meezan, W. (Eds.), *Child Welfare: Current Dilemmas. Future Directions*. Itasca, IL: F. E. Peacock Press.

Silbur, E. & Tippett, J. (1965). Self-Esteem: Clinical Assessment and Measurement Validation. *Psychological Reports*, 16, 1017-1071.

Simmons, R., Brown, L., Bush, D. & Blyth, D. (1978). Self-Esteem of Black and White Adolescents. *Social Problems*, 26, 86-96.

Simpson, C., & Boyal, D. (1975). Esteem Construct Generality and Academic Performance. *Educational and Psychological Measurement*, 35, 897-907.

Solarz, A. (1988). *Homelessness: Implications for Children and Youth. Social Policy Report for Society forr Research in Child Development*, 3(4).

Solarz, A., Mowbray, C., & Dupuis, S. (1986*). Michigan Human Services Task Force on the Homeless: Executive Summary and Report.* Lansing: Michigan Department of Mental Health.

Spillane-Grieco, E. (1984). Feelings and Perceptions of Parents of Runaways. *Child Welfare*, 63, 159-166.

St. Louis, M., Hayman, C., Miller, C., Anderson, J., Peterson, L., & Dondero, T. (1989). HIV Infection in Disadvantaged Adolescents in the U.S.: *Findings From the JOB Corps Screening Program. Abstracts of the V International Conference on AIDS*, Ottawa, Ontario, Canada: International Research Development Center, 711.

Stefanidis, N., Pennbridge, J, Mackenzie, R. and Pottharst, K. (1992) Runaway and Homeless Youth: the Effects of Attachment History on Stabilization. *American Journal of Orthopsychiatry* 62(3) 442-446

Stricof, R., Novick, L. & Kennedy, J. (1990). *HIV-1 Seroprevalence in Facilities for Runaway and Homeless Youth in Four States: Florida, Texas, Louisiana, and New York.* Paper Presented at the Sixth International Conference on AIDS, San Francisco, CA.

Swenson, C. (1979). Social Networks, Mutual Aid, and the Life Model of Practice. In Germaine, C. (Ed*.), Social Work Practice:*

People and Environments. New York: Columbia University Press.

Taylor, D., Biafora, F., and Warnheit, G. (1994) Racial Mistrust and Disposition to Deviance among African-American, Haitian, and Other Caribbean Adolescent Boys. Special Issue: Race, Ethnicity, and the Law. *Law and Human Behavior* 18 (3) 291-303

Taylor, R. (1976). Psychosocial Development among Black Children and Youth: A Re-Examination. *American Journal of Orthopsychiatry*, 46, 4-19.

Teare,J. Furst, D, Peterson, R, and Authier, K. (1992) Family Reunification Following Shelter Placement: Child, Family, and Program Correlates. *American Journal of Orthopsychiarty* 62(1) 142-146

Teri, L. (1982). Depression in Adolescence: Its Relationship to Assertion and Various Aspects of Self Image. *Journal of Clinical Child Psychology*, 2, 101-106.

Teri, L. (1982). The Use of the Beck Depression Inventory with Adolescents. *Journal of Abnormal Child Psychology*, 10, 277-284.

Thoits, P. (1983). Conceptual, Methodological, and Theoretical Problems in Studying Social Support as a Buffer Against Life Stress. *Journal of Health and Social Behavior*, 23, 565-575.

Tolsdorf, C. (1976). Social Networks, Support, and Coping. *Family Process*, 15, 407-417.

United States Bureau of Census (1987). Money, Income, and Poverty Status of Families and Persons in the United States: 1986. *Current Population Reports*, (Series P-60) 157, Washington DC.

United States Department of Health and Human Services Office of Human Development Services Administration of Children Youth and Families (1984). *Runaway Youth Centers: FY 1984 Report to Congress*, 1984, Washington D.C.

United States General Accounting Office. (1989). *Homeless and Runaway Youth Receiving Services at Federally Funded Shelters*. Report to the Honorable Paul Simon, United States Senate, Washington, DC.

Van Houten, T. & Golembriewski, G. (1978). *Adolescent Life Stress as a Predictor of Alcohol Abuse and/or Runaway Behavior*. Washington, DC: Youth Alternatives Project.

Vaux, A. & Harrison, D. (1985). Social Network Characteristics Associated with Support Satisfaction and Perceived Support. *American Journal of Community Psychology*, 13(3), 245-268.

Vaux, A. , Riedel, S. & Stewart, D. (1987). Modes of Social Support: The Social Support Behaviors Scale. *American Journal of Psychology*, 15, 209-237.

Vernon, S. & Roberts, R. (1982). Use of SADS-RDC in Tri-Ethnic Community Survey. *Archives of General Psychiatry*, 39, 47-52.

Vik, P., Grizzle, K, and Brown, S. (1992) Social Resource Characteristics and Adolescent Substance Abuse Relapse. *Journal of Adolescent Chemical Dependency* 2 (2) 59-74

Vondra, J. & Garbarino, J. (1988). Social Influences on Adolescent Behavior Problems. In Salzinger, S., Antrobus, J., & Hammer, M. (Eds.), *Social Networks of Children, Adolescents, and College Students*. Hillsdale, NJ: Lawrence Erlbaum Associates.

Warren, J. Gary, F. , and Moorhead, J. (1994) Self-Reported Experiences of Physical and Sexual Abuse among Runaway Youths. *Perspectives in Psychiatric Care* 30(1) 23-28

Weiss, R. (1991). The Attachment Bond in Childhood and Adulthood. In Parks, C., Stevenson-Hinde, J. & Marris, P. (Eds.), *Attachment Across the Life Cycle*. New York: Tavistock/Rutledge.

Wenet, G. (1979). *Life Stress and the Adolescent Sex Offender: A Comparative Study*. Unpublished Manuscript, University of Washington.

White, R. (1974). Strategies of Adaptation: An Attempt at Systematic Description. In Coehlo, G., Hamburg, D., & Adams, J. *Coping and Adaptation*. New York: Basic Books.

Wiltse, K. (1985). Foster Care; An Overview. In Laird, J. & Hartman, A. (Eds.), *A Handbook of Child Welfare: Context, Knowledge, and Practice*. New York: Free Press.

Wyche, K. & Rotheram-Borus, M. (1990). Suicidal Behavior among Minority Youth In the United States. In Stiffman, A. & Davis, L. (Eds.), *Ethnic Issues In Adolescent Mental Health*. Newbury, CA: Sage Publications.

Yates, G., Mackenzie, R., Pennbridge, J., & Cohen, E. (1988). A Risk Profile Comparison of Runaway and Non-Runaway Youth. *American Journal of Public Health*, 78, 820-821.

Zelnick, M. & Shah, F. (1983). First Intercourse among Young Americans. *Family Planning Perspectives*, 15, 64-70.

Zide, M. and Cherry, A. (1992) A Typology of Runaway Youths: Empirically Based Definition. *Child and Adolescent Social Work Journal* 9(2) 155-168

Zimet, G., Sobo, E., Zimmerman, T., and Jackson, J., Sexual Behavior, Drug Use, Aids Knowledge among Midwestern Runaways. *Youth and Society* 26(4) 450-462

Zimmerman, M. and Maton, K. (1992) Life-Style and Substance Abuse among African-American Urban Adolescents: A Cluster Analytic Approach. *American Journal of Community Psychology* 20 (1), 121-138

Zimmerman, R. (1988). Childhood Depression: New Theoretical Formulations and Implications for Foster Care Services. *Child Welfare*, 63(1), 37-46.

Index

Please remember that this is a library book,
and that it belongs only temporarily to each
person who uses it. Be considerate. Do
not write in this, or any, library book.